Beyond the Classroom

Go beyond the walls of your classroom to build literacy and achievement. In this insightful book, you'll discover how you can better meet the rigorous goals of the Common Core by opening new lines of communication with colleagues, parents, and students. Each chapter centers around an action project that was designed to help teachers improve literacy by moving beyond the typical class lessons and worksheets. The projects include:

- A book club for families of kindergarten and first grade students, to help students build foundational literacy skills
- A book club designed to engage middle school students with young adult literature using digital forums
- "Write with your child" evenings to help parents connect with their middle school children
- An instructional team's challenge to use a range of mentor texts in their classrooms
- And much more!

As you read each project, you'll come away with ideas and inspiration that you can apply to your own teaching. By challenging yourself to connect with parents and colleagues on a deeper level, you will be better able to align your work, adjust for your students, and achieve your teaching goals.

Nanci Werner-Burke is a former middle and high school teacher. She directs the Endless Mountains Writing Project (an affiliate of the National Writing Project) and is a professor at Mansfield University.

Other Eye on Education Books Available from Routledge
(www.routledge.com/eyeoneducation)

Rebuilding Research Writing
Strategies for Sparking Informational Inquiry
Nanci Werner-Burke, Karin Knaus, and Amy Helt DeCamp

Writing Behind Every Door
Teaching Common Core Writing in the Content Areas
Heather Wolpert-Gawron

Common Core in the Content Areas
Balancing Content and Literacy
Jessica Bennett

Nonfiction Strategies That Work
Do This—Not That!
Lori G. Wilfong

Vocabulary Strategies That Work
Do This—Not That!
Lori G. Wilfong

The Common Core Grammar Toolkit
Using Mentor Texts to Teach the Language Standards in Grades 6–8
Sean Ruday

The Common Core Grammar Toolkit
Using Mentor Texts to Teach the Language Standards in Grades 3–5
Sean Ruday

Family Reading Night, Second Edition
Darcy J. Hutchins, Marsha D. Greenfeld, and Joyce L. Epstein

Focus on Text
Tackling the Common Core Reading Standards, Grades 4–8
Amy Benjamin

Flipping Your English Class to Reach All Learners
Strategies and Lesson Plans
Troy Cockrum

Create, Compose, Connect! Reading, Writing, and Learning with Digital Tools
Jeremy Hyler and Troy Hicks

Beyond the Classroom

Collaborating with Colleagues and Parents to Build Core Literacy

Edited by
Nanci Werner-Burke

NEW YORK AND LONDON

First published 2015
by Routledge
711 Third Avenue, New York, NY 10017

and by Routledge
2 Park Square, Milton Park, Abingdon, Oxon, OX14 4RN

Routledge is an imprint of the Taylor & Francis Group, an informa business

© 2015 Taylor & Francis

The right of the editor to be identified as the author of the editorial
material, and of the authors for their individual chapters, has been asserted in
accordance with sections 77 and 78 of the Copyright, Designs and Patents
Act 1988.

All rights reserved. No part of this book may be reprinted or reproduced or
utilized in any form or by any electronic, mechanical, or other means, now
known or hereafter invented, including photocopying and recording, or in any
information storage or retrieval system, without permission in writing from
the publishers.

Trademark notice: Product or corporate names may be trademarks or registered
trademarks, and are used only for identification and explanation without
intent to infringe.

Library of Congress Cataloging-in-Publication Data
Beyond the classroom : collaborating with colleagues and parents to build core
   literacy / edited by Nanci Werner-Burke.
      pages cm
   Includes bibliographical references.
   1. Language arts (Early childhood)—Social aspects—United States.
2. Literacy—Social aspects—United States.   3. Language arts—Standards—
United States.   4. Language arts—Curricula—United States.   5. Community
and school.   6. Education—Parent participation.   7. Home and school.
I. Werner-Burke, Nanci.
   LB1576.B4924 2014
   372.6—dc23
   2014012930

ISBN: 978-1-138-01609-5 (hbk)
ISBN: 978-1-138-01610-1 (pbk)
ISBN: 978-1-315-79397-9 (ebk)

Typeset in Bembo
by Apex CoVantage, LLC

Printed and bound in the United States of America by Publishers Graphics,
LLC on sustainably sourced paper.

Contents

	Meet the Author	*vii*
1	Extraordinary Measures NANCI WERNER–BURKE	1
2	Reading Connections: Building a Partnership Between Families and School JESSICA SPENCER	9
3	Digital Connections: Turn Ravenous Readers into Sophisticated Discussion Leaders MELISSA MORRAL	27
4	Writing Connections: The Not-So-Secret Mission of Parental Involvement BOBBI BUTTON	43
5	Connecting the Curriculum: Some Book on Cambodia KARIN KNAUS AND STACEY SEGUR	55
6	Connecting Teachers with Authentic Texts JANE M. SPOHN	69
7	Connecting Content: The True Story of Dead End CINDY LISOWSKI	83
8	Connecting Teachers: Teaming up for Essential Vocabulary JULIE WEAVER	97
9	Conclusion: Let There Be Light: Where Will You Connect? NANCI WERNER–BURKE	119

Appendix A: In November *Newsletter*	*123*
Appendix B: Animalia *Newsletter*	*125*
Appendix C: All the Water in the World *Newsletter*	*127*
Appendix D: Teacher Questionnaire	*129*
Appendix E: Parent Questionnaire	*131*
Appendix F: EUREKA Flyer	*133*

Meet the Author

Nanci Werner-Burke is a certified reading specialist and grade 7–12 English teacher, as well as a full professor at Mansfield University in Pennsylvania. She is the director of the Endless Mountains Writing Project, lead author of the book *Rebuilding Research Writing: Strategies for Sparking Informational Inquiry* (2014), and earned a PhD in English from Indiana University of PA. She has contributed work to *Educational Leadership, PA Reads, Voices from the Middle,* and the *Keystone Reader.* Nanci lives in a cabin, in a wood, with her wonderful 8-year old. She is a full professor at Mansfield University of Pennsylvania.

Contributors

Bobbi Button began her teaching preparation at Mansfield University, earning a BS in English Education and going on to earn an MA in Creative Writing at Wilkes University. She is certified to teach language arts, social sciences, and drive a big rig. Bobbi lives with her family on a dairy farm in rural Pennsylvania. She strives to ignite her students' passion for writing daily.

Karin Knaus holds a BA in Speech Communication and Psychology from Susquehanna University and earned her teaching certification for grades 7–12 English and a Master of Science in Education degree in K–12 literature at Mansfield University. She is a co-author of the book *Rebuilding Research Writing: Strategies for Sparking Informational Inquiry* (2014). Karin is an English teacher, writer, and sometimes stage actress who is passionate about the very nerdy researching of research writing. When she isn't in the classroom, she may be found entertaining her nieces, driving on a back road, or trying out a new recipe in her mom's kitchen.

Cindy Lisowski is a certified educator in secondary English and library media. She holds a BSE in English from Mansfield University and an MSE in English from Elmira College. At the age of five, she discovered she loved going to school and has not stopped since. A lifelong letter writer and reader, she is currently building individual libraries for her grandchildren. She is passionate about dancing, shopping, cooking, and great coffee.

Melissa Morral holds teaching certifications in elementary school and special education, as well as middle school language arts and social studies. She has earned a Bachelor of Science in Education from Mansfield University, a master's degree from Gannon University, and has contributed to *Voices from the Middle*.

Stacey Segur, a senior English teacher of 17 years, is a member of national and state professional organizations, and is a leader in school and community activities. She earned a Master of Science in Education degree from Wilkes University and is certified to teach secondary language arts and social studies. When not grading papers, she enjoys walking, swimming, reading, and watching movies.

Jessica Spencer holds teaching certifications in environmental education, ESL, general science, and middle level citizenship, and is a reading specialist. She earned a Bachelor of Science in Environmental Science degree from Dickinson College and a Master of Science in Education degree from Mansfield University.

Jane M. Spohn is certified to teach elementary education, middle school math, and science, and is a reading specialist. She has earned bachelor's and master's degrees in education from Mansfield University. Always on the prowl for an engaging read for herself or her students, Jane teaches and lives in a literary paradise. As a wife, mother of four, grandmother, mentor, friend, Girl Scout leader, and Sunday school teacher, humor is her best friend.

Julie Weaver came to the field of teaching from the oil and gas business, in which she worked as a petroleum exploration geologist for 6 years. She holds a BA in Geology from Amherst College and earned her teaching certifications for elementary education, grades 7–12 earth and space science, and general science, and a Master of Science in Elementary Education degree at Mansfield University. Julie has currently found her home in the fourth grade after having taught in various grades from 4 through 11 in her 26-year teaching career. Julie's first published article came out in her favorite publication, *Science and Children*, in 2010. Julie won a Presidential Award for Excellence in Science Teaching in 1995.

CHAPTER

Extraordinary Measures
Nanci Werner-Burke

Magical Beginnings

Before you start to read this book, let's write. You can use the margins, a piece of scrap paper, or your journal. Take at least 10 minutes to write your response as you consider the following:

If you had a magic wand and could make three educational wishes, what changes would you make for/to

1. *your students,*
2. *your colleagues, and*
3. *your community?*

This prompt is one I have used, with variation, in professional development sessions with fellow educators. Always, we answer it in writing, and usually, in the ensuing discussion, after a bit of sharing and some griping and complaining, we move to a place in the conversation where we start to discover ways to move these changes from a wish list into reality.

It was one of these sessions that grew and morphed into the collection of seven action research projects that make up this book. Teachers tend to gripe and worry about the three things that are at the heart of the writing prompt: how they can engage and motivate their students, have more effective relationships with their colleagues, and strengthen how their community views their school.

It is an easy trap to get caught up in: lamenting in a dire tone that students don't care because their parents don't do enough to support the school's mission or that you are only one teacher and can only do so much. It's also self-defeating. Argue for your limitations and sure enough, they're all yours. In our workshops, after allowing an appropriate amount of time for venting, we take a right turn and move away from seeing these issues as problems that can never be solved. We begin to look into the reasons and causes behind them, and start to look for steps that will lead to positive change.

Our answers may not be your answers. The authors who have contributed to this collection are all teacher consultants (TCs) for the Endless Mountains Writing Project, a site of the National Writing Project (nwp.org) that is hosted by the Department of Education and Special Education at Mansfield University of Pennsylvania. These projects do not come from a sense of desperation over the state of education. These projects come from a place of strength. They are models of what is possible, of what leadership looks like.

These projects came at a point when these TCs had been involved with the Endless Mountains Writing Project for a number of years and had been working steadily on revamping and enhancing their classroom practices. All have earned graduate degrees in areas related to their fields, and they are truly master teachers in their classrooms. Writing is prominent in their pedagogy, classroom practices, and work with students. While their teaching techniques did not become static while they were working on these projects, it is worth noting that they were challenged at the outset to identify a need and undertake a project that would push them in some way to make an impact on literacy *outside* of the traditional classroom setting and schedule. This book was aimed at the outset at finding ways to think outside the classroom box and move their work beyond the door of their classroom settings.

So, to be clear, these are the voices of real teachers. They stand in front of (and behind, and next to) their K–12 students each school day (and after, during extracurricular athletics and clubs, in the grocery store, in church, and at the movies). Their projects have unfolded in public schools in the Canton, Northern Tioga, and Southern Tioga School Districts—strong districts in northeastern Pennsylvania that have empowered their teachers to build core literacy skills across content areas and grade levels. Rather than being asked to follow a prescriptive program, these teachers were charged with finding ways to think *beyond* the parameters of classroom instruction and build connections with students, parents, and other educators. If you are looking for a quick collection of activities to try out with your own students, you won't find that here. This collection is focused on how teachers can improve student learning by going beyond the teacher-student paradigm and building connections in places and spaces not previously utilized.

This book goes past the context of the classroom and explores how teachers can open new lines of communication with colleagues, parents, and students. The goal was to improve achievement by developing the communication and cognition-based foundations for literacy though multiple aspects and outreach. Our site projects represented the opportunity to step back and look at our schools and students with fresh eyes. Each initiative developed from efforts that were purposeful and goal-driven, but those efforts centered on responding to the different needs and opportunities each teacher saw. Our projects allowed these teachers, who were already identified as being innovative, successful educators constantly honing their craft, to re-envision their roles as teachers and recognize other paths to student success. This text delineates how these plans unfolded and spread in impact.

Our work brought us together, for face-to-face meetings and online work sessions, for well over a year. During that year, in true Writing Project fashion, it was a combination of passion for our work, a love for our students, and professional and personal fellowship that kept us going. Whether slogging in through snow to make use of a school holiday to make progress on the manuscript or closing the window shades in the computer lab in an effort to ignore the beautiful summer weather that tempted us away from our keyboards, each of these teachers persevered to make their projects successful. Meeting together helped us share our successes and address our obstacles. Karaoke-rapping about topics, canoeing across Pine Creek, and roller-derby style basketball helped us get past the stress and take ourselves a little less seriously over the years we have spent working together.

And, yes, there has been a great deal of stress. Change is a constant in many fields and areas, but in education, it sometimes seems as though there is a competition to see how many changes and course-reversals it will take to push good teachers out of the profession. It is worth acknowledging that this book may not have been written and the projects not undertaken if we had waited a few years, as the pressure has been mounting on teachers in unprecedented ways and from multiple directions.

Our State of Change: A (Common)wealth

While we all place pressure on and push ourselves to move forward in our teaching craft, the amount of external elements that also function in this role are increasing, both in our state and across the country.

Pennsylvania is a state with two high-stakes tests; the Pennsylvania System of School Assessment (PSSA) is currently administered at checkpoints in the elementary and middle school grades, and encompasses the areas of reading, math, writing, and science. Passing the Keystone Exam, which focuses on specific content-area knowledge, is currently an exit exam for the high school level. The PDE (Pennsylvania Department of Education) recently has made student scores on these exams a part of how public school teachers and districts will be evaluated. It is perhaps a natural consequence of the digital information age that our society has become focused on collecting data and performance metrics. However, it is easy to lose balance on the slippery slope of analysis and become so focused on raising test scores that we lose the bigger picture of helping students to think and feel and process their worlds.

This book was undertaken with the perspective that educators benefit from having a common framework of goals to work toward, and that collaboration and communication can only benefit teachers. We believe that these goals must be in line with what our students will need to think and communicate effectively, to get the most out of their lives, contribute to society positively, and make a living. When our state adopted the Common Core (www.corestandards. org), and set a timeline to integrate it into all public school districts, we realized that we would need to dive into the Common Core documents and educate ourselves on what they were and said, and to see if there were overlaps with our beliefs or a total disjuncture.

When we unpacked the actual Common Core ELA standards, we began to recognize that *many of the core goals are an extension of what good teachers have been striving for all along.* Others are questionable, perhaps unattainable at the grade levels to which they have been aligned, but have at least functioned to open the door to professional discussions and debates that would not have otherwise occurred.

If you already made your peace with the Common Core, you are aware that the standards set high goals that require students to problem-solve by reading multiple, increasingly complex texts capably, and by formulating cohesive written responses. The importance of these skills is hard to argue with in our text-drenched, information-heavy society. To make progress toward these goals, teachers must be empowered to explore teaching methods and practices that will align their efforts and overcome obstacles. They must reach out and connect with real-world home and community resources, and build capacity and support structures there. In this way, our work in this book is aligned with the Common Core.

If you are not a fan of the Common Core, well, okay. Some states and districts have responded to the Common Core State Standards (CCSS) by adopting heavily scripted programs that support the notion of commonality in terms of providing homogeneous instruction targeted at preparing students to perform on standardized assessments. While we recognize that standardized assessment can be useful for comparing districts and states, our work was aimed not specifically at raising test scores or standardizing our approaches. This is one reason you will not find black-line masters or fill-in-the-template handouts in this book. Just as we are asking students to think at new levels and problem-solve with evidence and creativity, the bar is being raised for teachers to do this, as well. You will not find scripts with a "sure fire" claim that if you replicate exactly what these teachers did, your work will be a slam-dunk success. Such a claim would not be credible when working with real people, in real settings.

Each teacher looked carefully at their own situation and context, and utilized surveys and other means of data collection to help shape their steps throughout the process. Our examples serve to help you find your own departure point and set your own path, which is, after all, what real teachers do. Mine the data and keep the people in mind and you will have a plan that is best-suited for making a difference at your own site.

What Else Can I Do?

Good teaching in the classroom makes a difference. *But . . .* what happens in the classroom space and time is only one aspect of educating a child. In our projects, we covered seven strands of action research that were designed to explore how these educators could move their students toward high-order thinking and literacy development by going beyond the constraints of the traditional classroom. Our goal in undertaking these projects was to develop a framework of options that teachers and administrators could utilize as they revamp their work for a 21st-century world. Each chapter provides a protocol of guiding questions and points for educators to consider as they read about the different projects and consider what choices fit best with their own students, schools, and communities.

The contributors have taken care to share their personal experiences and firsthand knowledge of their schools, students, and communities. This feature makes the work accessible, and asks you, the reader, to come into our worlds and stay there awhile. Each author's goals are clearly stated, and they provide an overview of their context that allows you to compare and contrast important elements with your own situation. In keeping with that aspect of the text, each chapter contains a section that provides connections to literature and research that delineates what the published work in our profession has to say about the related topic. Just as these authors share the successes and setbacks of their work, they have built their initiatives on what others have found and tried, and the literature review connects these pieces. The research review is your invitation to the larger professional conversation, and we hope that you accept it.

In each chapter, you will find the specific steps each investigator took, supported by actual examples from the different projects. The foundation is also laid for taking the work to a more complex level, and there are guiding questions and points for educators to consider as they read about the different projects and decide what choices fit best with their own students, schools, and communities.

It may be useful to think of the chapters in terms of the connections that are made in each one, and the prompt items they address. The first three in the collection document outreach to families and reaching out of the traditional teaching space and time as a means to engage students, families, and community members in the educational conversation.

Jessica Spencer focused on an outreach program for families of kindergarten and first grade students, in order to reach parents very early in the reading and writing process. Through a family literacy children's book club, teachers, students, and families were given an opportunity to connect with each other and specific texts to build a foundation of literacy skills. This project is delineated in Chapter 2, "Reading Connections: Building a Partnership Between Families and School."

Melissa Morral also implemented a book club, but connected middle school students with young adult (YA) literature using digital forums, which brought her work outside of the classroom and into extracurricular time. In Chapter 3, "Digital Connections: Turn Ravenous Readers into Sophisticated Discussion Leaders," she outlines her efforts to promote higher-order thinking and deepen reader interaction with YA texts by modeling increasingly complex questioning techniques. The result was not only better-prepared students, but also approaches that she was able to utilize in her in-class teaching time.

Chapter 4, by Bobbi Button, is titled, "Writing Connections: The Not-So-Secret Mission of Parental Involvement." This project combines the family outreach thread with a middle school demographic, but with a focus on connecting participants specifically through writing. Button reflects on her own experiences as a student and then as a teacher, and works to bridge the gap between the two, so that the parents of her students have the resources and tools to better engage with the direction of the school district.

The final four chapters collectively shift direction and focus on building teaching capacity through professional collaboration and curricular alignment. It seems particularly appropriate, given this focus, that Chapter 5, "Connecting the Curriculum: Some Book on Cambodia," represents the work of two authors, Stacey Segur and Karin Knaus, who teamed up to collaboratively investigate how research writing was being taught across the content areas in their respective buildings. This chapter follows their processes of identifying an area of need and working together to address it, despite differences in how their schools and schedules were structured.

Jane Spohn continues the cross-curricular approach in Chapter 6, "Connecting Teachers with Authentic Texts." Her chapter includes the steps she took to further engage an existing instructional team and motivate its members to experiment with using a range of mentor texts in their classrooms.

In Chapter 7, "Connecting Content: The True Story of Dead End," Cindy Lisowski also reaches out to a variety of content-area teachers, but with the intent of rallying them around one common mentor text: the award-winning novel, *Dead End in Norvelt*, by Jack Gantos.

Finally, Julie Weaver brings the collection to a close. Chapter 8, "Connecting Teachers: Teaming up for Essential Vocabulary," chronicles multiple teacher-development projects that have unfolded in her school since she became a teacher consultant for the Endless Mountains Writing Project. While each of these projects demonstrates what teachers can do when they are supported in their efforts to break new ground, this last chapter best exemplifies our Writing Project mission of bringing good teachers together and building capacity across classrooms, schools, and districts. What began as a five-part series of professional workshops at Julie's school gathered momentum and set off successive ways of teaching opportunities and engagement.

As you browse, skim, and, at points, closely read these chapters, you will find many departure points for new projects to try out. Be an active reader and thinker; don't discard a project because it is focused on middle school and you are teaching at the elementary level, for example. Keep your response to the three-wishes writing prompt at hand, and reflect on which areas have the greatest need and potential as you read. All of these approaches will take some effort; all will take some time. We urge you to take that time and commit to the effort, and to use this text as your been-there, tried-that guide. Make your wishes come true.

CHAPTER

2 Reading Connections
Building a Partnership Between Families and School

Jessica Spencer

"To learn to read is to light a fire; every syllable that is spelled out is a spark."
—Victor Hugo, *Les Miserables*

A Language All Its Own

Many of the words in this chapter title are "buzz" words that surround the teaching of reading and writing in our schools. As educators, we are all too familiar with the sounds of these words during faculty meetings, grade-level gatherings, and curriculum alignment sessions. We sit patiently, we smile, we nod, and then, somewhere in the room, the grumbling begins—the plea for help. "If only parents would do this at home." "If I only had a little bit of support outside of the classroom." "How am I supposed to motivate when I am the ONLY motivator?" Lucy Calkins calls the types of educators who take the complaining route "curmudgeons," but regardless of our stance, either we find a way to address these needs or find another place to eat lunch (Calkins, 2012, p. 11).

Parent involvement is a bit of a slippery slope. We want the students' parents to help, but we also want them helping in a way that will support and not defeat the lessons being taught in the classroom. Parents sometimes need help from the teacher. If I didn't work within the walls of education, I probably would be pretty confused with all the educational jargon that is sometimes spoken and written to parents. The whole process of reading might sound like a foreign language to parents sending their children off to kindergarten.

Dear Parent(s) and Guardian(s),

We are now starting the alphabetic principle in class, starting with the letter 's'. Please practice this letter at home with your child. Saying the sound of the letter and words that start with that sound will help build phonemic awareness . . .

Three red flags: (1.) alphabetic principle, (2.) start with the letter s, and (3.) phonemic awareness.

The letter may sound great to a kindergarten teacher or reading specialist, but not so much to mom and dad, who are trying to squeeze homework lessons in before dinner or after dinner and before bath and bedtime. Parents have plenty to do after school, and trying to decipher the intentions of the assignment can be difficult and eventually pushed back onto the teacher. So, getting parents involved may not always be simple. In this chapter, I will share how I set out to achieve quality parental involvement by setting up a family literacy children's book club. My goal was to do more than introduce the concepts behind these buzz words. I wanted to really help families read aloud with each other, and motivate them to continue their literacy journeys at home.

Let the Journey Begin

> Did you know that learning to read is a challenge for almost 40 percent of kids? The good news is that with early help, most reading problems can be prevented. The bad news is that 44 percent of parents who notice their child having trouble wait a year or more before getting help.
>
> (Reading Rockets, 2013)

My journey began with the idea to start a family literacy children's book club with kindergarten and first grade families to reach out to all levels of readers and writers. I chose three books, with various reading lessons, that families received throughout the school year. I handed out the books approximately 1 month in advance of the meetings, and they were sent home for them to keep. I chose the following books: *In November* by Cynthia Rylant, *Animalia* by Graeme Base, and *All the Water in the World* by George Ella Lyon. Each story was accompanied by a newsletter that included certain topics in reading, writing, discussion questions, activities, author biographies, further reading, and previews of the book that followed. Families then met at an elementary school library three times to discuss some of these topics, conduct an activity that I designed related to the book, and enjoy snacks and the company of each other.

The goals of the project were to get parents involved in the literacy development of their children, demonstrate a way for teachers to get parents involved, and motivate students and families to read together and do literacy-based activities at home. I worked with 4 kindergarten teachers, 4 first grade teachers, and 24 families that signed up for the book club. The elementary school involved was a K–6 school with 459 students. Just under half of the student population qualified for free and reduced lunch. The student to teacher ratio was 12:1.

For the Love of Learning

Family literacy programs have been promoted for more than 20 years. The aim of these various programs has been to enhance the literacy skills of students and their families at home (Caspe, 2003). Educators often complain that too many parents are not involved in their children's schooling, but what we really hope for is parents to be involved in their children's learning (Chasek & Rosen, 2011). Through a family literacy children's book club at the kindergarten and first grade level, teachers, students, and families are given an opportunity to come together to discuss reading and writing and build a foundation of literacy skills to last a lifetime.

Barbara Bush, the founder of the Barbara Bush Foundation of Family Literacy, states, "The home is the child's first school, the parent is the child's first teacher, and reading is the child's first subject" (Chance, 2010). Yet, according to the United States Department of Education, children are malnourished when it comes to the reading skills attained by kindergarten:

> If daily reading begins at infancy, by the time the child is 5 years old, he or she has been fed roughly 900 hours of brain food! Reduce that experience to just 30 minutes a week, and the child's hungry mind loses 770 hours of nursery rhymes, fairy tales, and stories. A kindergarten student who has not been read to could enter school with less than 60 hours of literacy nutrition. No teacher, no matter how talented, can make up for those lost hours of mental nourishment.
>
> (USDOE, 1999)

The relationship is evident. Parents who read frequently to their children give those children an added advantage when they enter school. The parents' role, power of choice, and structure at school play a major part in the value of reading and writing. Not only do we want our children to be good readers, but we also want them to enjoy reading and read for fun. Reading should be a passion that starts from the beginning for all kids to see. Being involved in a literacy project will hopefully close the gap for some of our learners and continue to expand young minds.

Children and parents agree that some of the most important outcomes of reading books come from reading for fun. Books open up their imagination, inspire them through characters and storylines, and provide new information

(Scholastic Media Room, 2010). As children age, there is a steady decline in reading for enjoyment, importance, and frequency. This is especially true among boys (KSRA, 2013). Parents play an important role in trying a variety of tactics to increase kids' time spent reading. Some of these tactics include choice, books in the home, limiting time with electronics and television, and books based on popular shows, movies, or toys (KSRA, 2013). Parents need to be aware of these findings and understand ways to continue to promote reading in the home.

The school plays an important role through offering opportunities for teachers and parents to work together for the common good of the student. The skills being focused on in class should transfer into the home, but if the parents are ill-equipped to support the skill, the partnership is damaged. Teaching parents ways in which to promote literacy at home helps to maintain and grow stronger learners. Showing parents how to conduct a read aloud, find a book that fits their child, and use discussion questions, connections, and activities themselves will help to foster this goal.

Parents also need to be aware of Common Core State Standards (CCSS) that will affect their child's education. Common Core Standards have set a new precedent in language arts in schools across the country. These standards serve parents by making it clear what their children should be learning and doing at a given level. In kindergarten, students will be expected to compare and contrast characters, link relationships between illustrations and text, and read with a purpose for both fiction and non-fiction texts (Pennsylvania Department of Education [PDE], 2010). Sight words, upper and lowercase words, segmentation, and long and short vowels should also be mastered (PDE, 2010). Finally, students should be writing every day and starting the peer view process (PDE, 2010).

When schools are preparing to make a shift in standards, it's a great time to re-examine approaches to family literacy. Emerging principles for family literacy programs are being developed in response to criticisms of family literacy programs of the past. New programs examine the specific needs of a community. They recognize the literacy history of parents attending, and provide an open dialogue in which parents contribute to the learning (Caspe, 2003). The literacy skills immediately needed in a rural area may differ from those that are needed by a child in an urban setting. Literacy is not as simple as learning to read and write. It encompasses social skills and is evolving to include the skills to function in a technological world.

High quality, effective family literacy programs focus on efforts that pertain to the entire family, are family centered, and are flexible in design with adaptive strategies (Swick, 2009). Family literacy is not a one-size-fits-all model.

Family literacy programs should address the specific needs of the community to help support, promote, and engage families.

Some states have long-existing family literacy programs, but others are developing centers for family involvement where parents and children are learning side by side. These new programs are focusing on process and discovery, rather than finding one right answer (Chasek & Rosen, 2011). The centers are setting up language arts activities that promote collaboration, critical thinking, creativity, and innovation. These activities are aligned to standards, and teachers are trained to facilitate and guide students and parents. "Students and parents communicate with one another as they learn to think critically, write clearly, evaluate, interpret, and appreciate the power of imagination and the impact of language, both print and digital, through fun, family oriented activities" (Chasek & Rosen, 2011). Lessons can be learned from such programs to find the right fit for an area that meets the needs of the students and the community.

Other programs, for example, Raising a Reader, focus their attention on children from birth to 5 years of age. Research emphasizes that this time is the "window of opportunity" for brain development in the area of language skills (Colburn, 2011). Programs are designed to get books in the home at a young age. In order to guarantee that the books are being used, Head Start, librarians, visiting nurses, and other partners serve as coordinators to help parents understand the importance of the program. Raising a Reader has made a specific difference with lower income families, as well as homes that do not have English as the first language (Colburn, 2011).

In my home state of Pennsylvania, our Keystone State Reading Association (KSRA), an affiliate of the International Reading Association (IRA), has proclaimed April as Families and Reading Month (KSRA, 2013). KSRA offers handouts that are free and reproducible for teachers, parents, and administrators. The first sentence of their letter home states, "Children develop a love of stories and poems when they read or are read to on a regular basis" (KSRA, 2013). This packet goes on to provide a calendar of reading and writing ideas and 15-minute activities for parents to do at home. Teachers can provide these calendars and packets to their students to get the ideas into the home, and maybe light a spark to get the reading ball rolling.

Reading and writing is a continuum that starts at birth and grows with us through adulthood. As we encounter stories, their words spread across the page and influence our decisions, discussions, and likes in this world. Stories serve as mentors as we play with words, create sentences, and learn to write. We are never too young or old to discover new books, new words, and new ideas.

Where the Rubber Meets the Road

Learning to read and write is an enormously complicated task. I decided to focus on kindergarten and first grade families in order to reach parents very early in the reading and writing process. I wanted to open up the children's book club to all parents and did not want to single out any one group of students at the school.

Administrators were contacted and made aware of the project and aims. Myself and six other teacher educators were attempting to conduct action research across school districts in rural north-central Pennsylvania that spanned from kindergarten to 12th grade. The research covered the topics of effective reading and writing strategies taking place across all content classrooms. We then waited for approval from the school board to go ahead with the project. Upon approval, I drafted a letter for my principal and described the intentions of the project I wanted to conduct at our elementary school, and asked for his support. He approved and the project was set to begin.

Next, I talked to the kindergarten and first grade teachers during our beginning-of-the-year DIBELS data meeting, in which we establish Tier 1, 2, and 3 students that qualify for Response to Intervention (RtI), and made them aware of the invitation that I wanted them to send home to the families. I also discussed the longevity of the project and goals to be accomplished. I wanted to invite kindergarten and first grade families to participate in a family literacy children's book club that would educate parents about the process of reading and writing, and motivate families to read together at home.

Invitations were sent out and the wait began. In two grades, with four sections apiece, twenty-four parents responded and said they were interested. I had 10 boys and 14 girls sign up. Now that I had my numbers, I put in my order for 24 copies for each of the three children's books. The Endless Mountain Writing Project (EMWP) provided the funding needed to purchase the books, which we ordered from a local bookstore in Wellsboro, Pennsylvania, called *From My Shelf Books*.

When the books arrived, I distributed our first text: *In November* by Cynthia Rylant. Each student received a book, a newsletter (see Appendix A), and a bookmark to take home. The newsletter provided the following information: advice on different strategies to use in reading and writing, discussion questions that went along with the story, activities, information about a Wikispace that I set up, author biography, further reading, and a preview of the next book to come. The date for our meeting was also presented in the newsletter. The bookmark had 10 ways for parents to read with their kids.

The first meeting was scheduled for November 19, which was right before Thanksgiving break. I had a very large turnout of 19 eager parents and kids. Discussion centered on the buzz words in reading and writing, and what teachers mean when they describe what is happening in the classroom. This meeting was predominantly parent focused, and more activities needed to be prepared for the kids. I chose *In November* for its repetition, and we discussed how repetition is important when choosing books. I displayed other books that emulated these traits (Figure 2.1), and how to choose books using the five finger rule. I also used the Reading Rockets website to walk parents through its Reading 101 section. This website offers a plethora of information about literacy for parents, teachers, administrators, and librarians. Finally, I showed parents the Wikispace that I had created, so they could link to information at home about literacy and have another resource for them and their children. I gave every family that evening a notebook to keep track of books they read together as a family and offered other handouts about reading strategies to try in the home.

After the first meeting, questionnaires were sent out to all eight elementary teachers (Appendix D). The purpose of the questionnaire was to discover teachers' expectations of parents about teaching reading and writing skills at home. It also addressed their strengths and struggles while teaching reading and writing in the classroom. Finally, it asked for ways to better improve the partnership between parents and teachers. I also developed a parent questionnaire, but held off handing out this to parents until our last meeting scheduled for March (Appendix E).

Figure 2.1 *In November* book club artifacts

The second meeting took place February 4, as I purposely left a gap after the winter break because of hectic schedules and winter weather. The second book, *Animalia* by Graeme Base, was sent home before the winter break, and families would have a month and a half to read the book and do the activities in the newsletter (Appendix B). I chose *Animalia* as an alphabet book for families to work on the alphabetic principle and have some fun at the same time. I also waited until halfway through the school year, so kindergarten participants would have had more exposure to these letters in class.

I wanted to make my second meeting more student-friendly and set it up so that the activities centered around the story (Figure 2.2). I had 12 families attend our second meeting. We discussed alliteration, and families competed to find as many items as they could from one of Graeme Base's pages for the letter D. Then students made animal masks based on one of the animals mentioned in the book (Figure 2.3). We wrapped up with a story, and this time, I gave families the third book, *All the Water in the World* by George Ella Lyon, and the newsletter that accompanied our text (Appendix C). The families that were not present received the book and newsletter the following day, after they were sent home with the students.

Figure 2.2 *Animalia* book club artifacts

Reading Connections

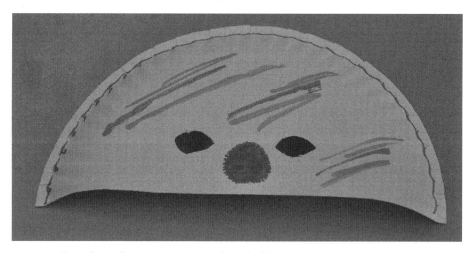

Figure 2.3 Sample student-created animal mask (lion)

Figure 2.4 *All the Water in the World* book club materials

I chose *All the Water in the World* to set up families for Poetry Month in April and Earth Day on April 22 (Figure 2.4). Our last meeting took place on March 4, and 14 parents attended. During our last meeting, we talked about onomatopoeia. We found onomatopoeia words in rain poetry, and students created an onomatopoeia story mobile that related to our story, *All the Water in the World* (Figure 2.5). On our last day, parents filled out a questionnaire about the program in which they had participated.

17

Figure 2.5 Student-created onomatopoeia rain mobile ("dot" and "spack")

Not only was I curious about teacher expectations, I also wanted the parents' perspectives, too. The parent questionnaire addressed their expectations of the teachers, and their strengths and weaknesses regarding reading and writing together as a family at home. Finally, I questioned their awareness of the Common Core Standards.

At the end of the week, prior to each meeting, I sent home a reminder of the time and place for our book club meeting to all families. For all three meetings, I provided food, drink, art supplies, and a prize to lure the families to come. The first prize was a random drawing for a $20 gas card; the second, a kid's bag full of activities, puzzles, and craft supplies; and, on the last night, every student received a bookmark, literacy dog tag, and candy-stuffed egg to take home because the spring break/Easter holiday arrived early at the end of March. I wanted every student to feel included and successful at the end of the program and end on a positive note to encourage participation the following year.

The Brass Tacks

Parent Data

Thirteen surveys were returned, and the responses revealed not a single parent was aware of the Common Core Standards and their potential to impact what is taught, learned, and assessed at school. I also found that most of the parents supported reading at home by taking time at bedtime to read to their child (Figure 2.6). Writing was supported in various ways, including creating stories, shopping lists, and thank you notes. Parents felt they needed more support or focus on writing, and time (Figure 2.7). The surveys reported that the parents

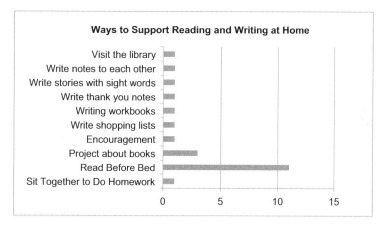

Figure 2.6 Parent survey results about supporting reading at home

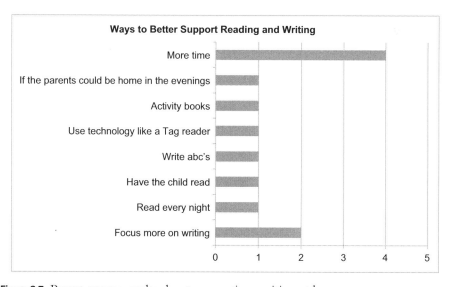

Figure 2.7 Parent survey results about supporting writing at home

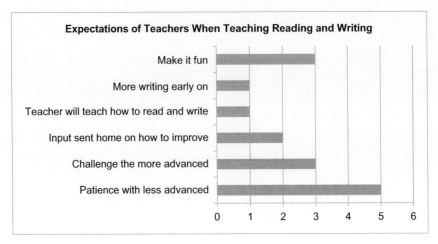

Figure 2.8 Parents' expectations of teachers

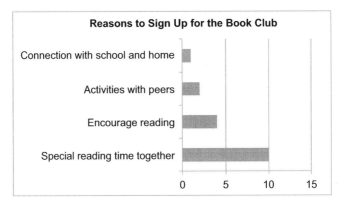

Figure 2.9 Reasons to sign up for the book club

expected patience from teachers while teaching reading and writing. They also wanted fun activities for their kids (Figure 2.8). Parents noted that it was important that the more advanced students also receive a challenge, and wanted to know what they could do to improve skills at home. Finally, the survey results showed that the parents overwhelmingly signed up for the book club to share a special reading time with their children (Figure 2.9). They thought it was valuable that it encouraged reading, was a peer-related activity, and connected school with home.

Teacher Data

Five surveys were returned from the eight teachers involved in the project. An analysis of the results showed that the teachers wanted parents to reinforce the skills being taught at school at home (Figure 2.10), and felt that more

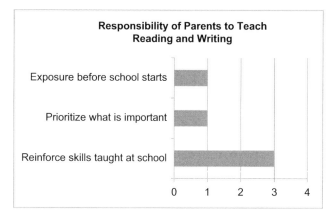

Figure 2.10 Teacher survey results about the responsibility of parents to teach reading and writing

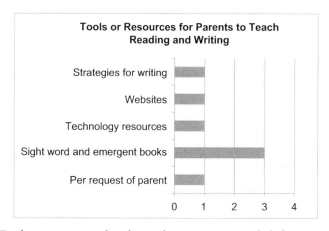

Figure 2.11 Teacher survey results about the resources needed for parents to better support reading and writing

sight word and emergent reader books should be made available to parents as a resource or tool to improve reading and writing at home (Figure 2.11). Technology was also mentioned, such as books on CD or e-readers, Tag reading systems, and websites offering reading and writing learning tools. Most teachers are confident in the sequential reading/phonics instruction, but varied with their struggles (Figure 2.12). Areas of struggle or difficulty included not feeling successful with all students, student readiness, class size for small group instruction, time, and re-teaching a skill that has been taught incorrectly (Figure 2.13).

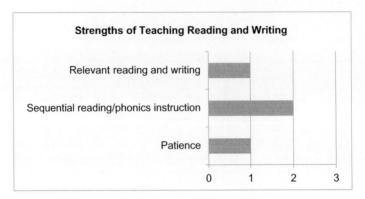

Figure 2.12 Teacher survey results about their teaching strengths

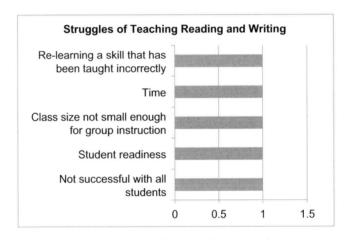

Figure 2.13 Teacher survey results about their teaching struggles

The responses indicated that the teachers were very much in favor of parent/teacher partnerships, but had varied opinions of involving parents in in-class projects, home/school folders, positive-news phone calls, and offering more programs like One School One Book at our elementary school (Figure 2.14). Every student in kindergarten through sixth grade receives the same book to read during January. The book is introduced with a school-wide assembly previewing and building background knowledge for the students. Parents and students have discussion questions each night after reading. Books can be part of the reading and language arts curriculum being taught in school. Finally, the project coincides and culminates with Family Reading Night at the school.

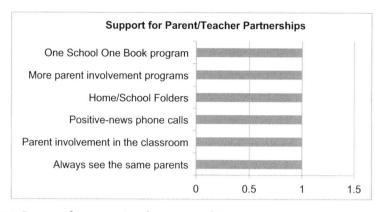

Figure 2.14 Support for parent/teacher partnerships

Parent Threads

The initial meeting with parents and laying the groundwork for the steps of the reading and writing process is very important for parents and children to hear and understand. I only spoke to 24 parents about this process. I feel that a literacy orientation should be conducted for all kindergarten and first grade families that addresses the steps in the process of learning how to read and write, and the steps that are taken throughout the school year to meet certain standards or benchmarks. I think this is especially true with the new Common Core Standards and the demand that will be placed on students to begin the reading and writing process very early in school. There needs to be a more clear expectation presented to parents about these standards and how school districts are handling this change.

The literacy event would be set up to speak to the parents separately during kindergarten orientation, while their children have the opportunity to play literacy games in another room or rooms. Kindergarten families would be addressed separately from first grade families by teachers at the school, reading specialists, and the principal. Then parents and children would be combined for another literacy activity to conclude the evening.

While speaking to the parents, they can be directed to multiple resources in which they can find information at school, in the community, and via the internet, where parents can go with any literacy questions. I feel that the family literacy night that happens halfway through the school year is a great motivator for parents and children to read and write together, but something needs to be accomplished earlier in the school year that sets parents and students up for success for the years to come.

I would like to see the family literacy children's book club continue for kindergarten and first grade students and families. I would provide the same setup for these families to get them to participate and attend such an event. Funding is an issue for this project to continue. Title I monies are available, but would have to be allocated for this to continue. If this was not an option, then grants would need to be pursued to supply books for each family.

Further research could provide more data to study the effect on student achievement. Are the students that attended the family literacy children's book club seeing an improvement in certain benchmarks and test scores? Are teachers seeing an improvement in attitude toward reading and writing in the classroom?

Getting all families involved is still the central struggle of family literacy. I believe this issue will continue to take program, teacher, school, and district efforts to supply multiple ways and resources to reach out to all families. It starts with reaching out when a child is born and getting books into the homes. It extends to preschool initiatives and preparation for kindergarten. It travels into the school district and the programs available from kindergarten through 12th grade, and back into the community where adult literacy programs need to be offered. Family literacy is a program with many dynamics that runs full circle from birth to adulthood. If the opportunities are available, advertised, supported, and conducted, then the hope is that families and students of varying backgrounds have the chance to succeed in the interlocking world of reading and writing.

Family Literacy Road Map

As delineated in this chapter, parent outreach can be an effective way for teachers to help support their students as they develop literacy skills. Additional materials, such as the newsletters that were sent home to parents and the surveys that were used with both teachers and parents, are available for your reference in the appendices. In addition, there are some more direct suggestions below for educators and administrators to guide their efforts.

Educators

Provide families with a handout of reading and writing buzz words and their definitions that teachers use every day. Also, provide a timeline of milestones to be reached in reading and writing throughout the school year. This might better convey to a parent the point their child will need to reach if they fall behind in a skill. I think educators do a great job communicating with parents, but phone calls and letters home may need to be updated to keep up with technology. Also, set up a grade-level Wikispace or link on the school website to post literacy information. Individual teachers could also maintain their own Wikispace or blog for parents to use at home.

Administrators

Allocate Title I monies for family literacy projects to begin or continue in the school districts. Organize literacy tips and expectations as part of kindergarten orientation, or create a separate night that solely addresses literacy for kindergarten and first grade families. Set up a book box outside of the main office door where families can drop off books and pick books up for free to use in their homes. Finally, allow time for teachers to plan and hold events to increase parent involvement and literacy initiatives at their schools.

(This chapter details the initial offering of this program. As we began the second offering in the 2013–2014 academic year, 42 families had already signed up to participate.)

References

Calkins, L. (2012). *Pathways to the common core: Accelerating achievement.* Portsmouth, NH: Heinemann.

Caspe, M. (2003, June). *Family literacy: A review of programs and critical perspectives.* Harvard Family Research Project, Cambridge, MA.

Chance, R. (2010). Family literacy programs—opportunities and possibilities. *Teacher Librarian, 37*(5), 8–12.

Chasek, A. S., & Rosen, M. (2011). Instilling a love of learning at home. *Education Digest, 77*(1), 57–61.

Colburn, N. (2011). Changing the world one bright red book bag at a time. *School Library Journal, 57*(9), 36–39.

Keystone State Reading Association (KSRA). (2013). *Families and Reading Month Packet.* Retrieved April 17, 2013, from http://ksrapa.org/?page_id=901

Pennsylvania Department of Education (PDE). (2010). *Pennsylvania common core standards.* Retrieved April 11, 2013, from www.pdesas.org/standard/commoncore

Reading Rockets. (2013). *Helping struggling readers.* Retrieved April 16, 2013, from www.readingrockets.org/helping/

Scholastic Media Room. (2010). *2010 kids and family reading report: Turning the page in the digital age.* Retrieved October 22, 2012, from http://mediaroom.scholastic.com/kfrr

Swick, K. J. (2009). Promoting school and life success through early childhood and family literacy. *Early Childhood Education Journal, 36,* 403–406.

United States Department of Education (USDOE). (1999). *National center for family literacy: Statistics.* Retrieved October 22, 2012, from www.famlit.org/media-resources/statistics

CHAPTER

Digital Connections
Turn Ravenous Readers into Sophisticated Discussion Leaders
Melissa Morral

Small Talk

It is lunchtime at a north-central rural Pennsylvania public school. Kids have carried their packed lunches and trays to my classroom to discuss *Divergent*, a book by Veronica Roth.

The discussion begins:

"I loved the book!"

"Me, too!"

"Best. Book. Eva!"

In many ways, the extracurricular book club I had started with my students was a teacher's dream. The students were avid readers who were so motivated by the books I dangled in front of them that they signed up voluntarily and were willing to devote a lunch period to talking about what they were reading. However, I found quickly that the depth of discussion was a serious problem. When we first began, conversation went nowhere. The kids were ravenous readers, but when it came to discussing the books, they waited for me to ask the questions. There were times when I felt like I was a dentist trying to extract the molar of a reluctant child. Trying to pry open their thoughts proved difficult. Their answers generally were basic, and only occasionally would a deep insight develop.

I was pretty certain if I could crack the code of preteen silence, these students would be well on their way toward developing the type of extended thinking skills that would benefit them later in school and in daily life. I knew what I wanted: discussions that looked more "real life"; higher-level, deeper questions and discussions; and students who draw from their memories, personal experiences, and thoughts on topics and themes. I also knew that developing these literacy habits would help them improve their scores on the standardized state tests, but getting there was going to prove challenging.

Getting depth in the discussions of my book club did not happen overnight. Developing depth was my purpose, achieved by making intentional instructional choice. I had to purposely construct steps to conducting discussions with depth. That meant that I, as their teacher, would need to look at how I had set up the club and take steps to widen my teaching perspective so that I would be better prepared to make the changes I needed to get the results I wanted.

Taking on "Assumicide"

> "The skills students develop in discussion will be with them all of their lives."
> —Cynthia Barry, "From Great Texts—to
> Great Thinking" (2010, p. 44)

In this chapter, I will detail the major issues I encountered when running my book club. I found students participated easily in discussions if there were someone to take the lead. Often, this was done by me, the teacher. How could I have students take the initiative and take turns being the discussion leader? When students ask deeper questions, we know that student engagement increases and their learning reaches new depths (Rothstein & Santana, 2011). What paths could I take to get them to ask deeper-meaning questions? These two goals merged into a model that I researched and fine tuned as I worked weekly with the two dozen or so seventh and eighth grade students that turned out for my book club.

A key figure in guiding my work was Kelly Gallagher. In his book, *Deeper Reading,* Gallagher talks about "assumicide," which he defines as the death of reading when it is assumed students possess the skills necessary to reach deeper levels of reading (Gallagher, 2004, p. 104). The first step to solving this problem was admitting that I was part of the problem.

My assumption that they could ask deeper questions on their own without support and practice was part of the massacre! I thought that because these kids loved to read, and read at high rates about deep topics, they were equipped to also discuss the topics they were reading.

Listening and discussion skills are major players in developing thinking and communication skills. Making sure students have opportunities to practice listening and discussion skills is not enough. Providing opportunities to practice these skills with rigor and depth are important, and I set out to uncover the ways that I, as a teacher, could accomplish this.

Fanning the Flames

There are four key areas I identified as having potential as I tackled these goals: motivation, book club structure, listening and speaking activities, and digital writing. McGaha and Igo (2012) discovered that actively cultivating student interest resulted in a higher turnout for their summer reading program, and their work nudged me to reconsider the way I was currently running my club. We met weekly during the school year and biweekly over summer break, but I wanted to bridge that gap between meetings. Cassandra Scharber (2009, p. 433) suggested, "Online book clubs are fun, engaging, and convenient activities for preteens and teens and are viewed by both parents and librarians as motivating and flexible." Perfect. I needed both students and parents on board. It was time to take my club on the road—the information superhighway. I was particularly interested in finding ways to use the internet to supplement those meetings and continue the dialogue beyond my classroom, to encourage discussion outside of the face-to-face meetings.

So, I had students who were interested and I had opened the door to participation a bit wider by thinking about expanding the talk online, but I knew that having *good* conversations would be both the key to keeping the students on board and in actually accomplishing something in the discussions. I found additional support for my focus on speaking and listening skills in the Common Core ELA standards my state had just adopted, and specific guidance in the work of Silver, Dewing, and Perini (2012). They state, "Effective oral communication is a crucial 21st century skill" (p. 37) and unpack this assertion by delineating three essential criteria for successful discussions: a high degree of student participation, a strong focus on essential content, and high levels of thinking (p. 39). In addition, the works of Kinser (2011), Hathaway (2011), Gambrell (2011), and Barry (2010) all address how viewing the reading process as a social activity can help students think about the topics at a deeper level.

Richetti and Sheerin (1999) informed my approach to questioning strategies. Teaching students about what kinds of questions elicit deeper meaning was key. I call this approach "sophisticated discussion." This type of discussion reaches beyond the mundane and almost cliché questions like, "What is your favorite part of the book?" or "Who was your favorite character and why?" Sophisticated discussion questions would encourage participants to make connections with their lives, with the world at large, and even with other texts drawing on themes, inferences, and critical thinking.

With all this in mind, I thought about how my students regularly used texting, instant messaging, and social networks to communicate. Writing, for adolescents who live in an age of digital communication, has taken on new importance and plays a prominent role in the way they socialize, share information, and structure their communication (Sweeny, 2010, p. 121), but many students don't recognize these tasks as writing (p. 124). If we supplemented our face-to-face meetings with online work, the line between oral discussion and written communication could be crossed, teaming up for a powerful way to document our discussions and build on them.

Discussion Etiquette

Before I began this aspect of my project, I needed some information about my students. In providing them with a survey, I found out some interesting tidbits. Half (50%) of the students in the club (22 surveys were completed) joined because they like to read, 23% heard the book club was fun, 23% had friends who joined, and 4% wanted to improve their reading skills. The majority (70%) of the students learned to enjoy reading at a very early age (0–5) while 18% began enjoying reading at ages 5–10. Surprisingly, 12% of the students who said they were 10 or older before they learned to enjoy reading.

Most of the students surveyed said they talk to their family and friends about the books they read. Most of them had never kept a reading journal, and very few of them used social networking to talk about the books they read. When discussing their books with other people, the students reported they like to recall the events of the books (40%), analyze the plot (25%), review the book in whole (15%), analyze the main characters (10%), and personally respond to the book (10%) (Figure 3.1).

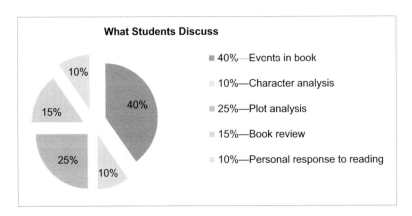

Figure 3.1 Students self-report what they focus on in book discussions

Throughout the course of working on this project, I was able to identify specific areas that my students were lacking in discussion skills. Once I introduced the skills necessary to conduct good discussions, the number of questions *I* needed to ask the group to keep the discussion going immediately went down. During the baseline, I was asking about 80% of the discussion questions. On average, after teaching how to ask good discussion questions, my lead in the discussion went down 55%.

Other notable improvements came in the transferring of the leadership role. I found that the more examples I provided (important to note, this occurred multiple times at each meeting), the more of a leadership role the students took in the discussion. Moreover, as I encouraged student discussion through modeling, the examples of discussion on the multiple levels of a text increased. For example, I found they were discussing plot, relationships, conflicts, themes, elements of a story, character development, analysis of point of view, comparing and contrasting the text with other texts, and so on.

In evaluating the types of questions asked, I used the revised Bloom's Taxonomy (Cochran, 2007) to categorize both the student contributions and my own (see Figure 3.2). While students held high averages of remembering kinds of questions, they rested comfortably in the analyzing and evaluating range of questions by the end of the project.

Perhaps the most important piece of literature I found pertaining to my project was John Spencer's *10 Ways to Help Students Ask Better Questions* (2011). I knew how to teach students how to *identify* good questions, but I wanted to extend that and teach them how to *construct* good questions. Spencer suggests teachers should first teach students to use questioning before, during, and after reading. Providing feedback and modeling good discussion questions that provide firm examples from which they can work can help them make the transition into constructing good questions in discussions.

To begin, I utilized both original and pre-written discussion questions to provide models for students. Then I used partially constructed questions to help guide them, and offered encouragement and suggestions for writing their own sophisticated questions. It was important to get the students to practice the skill of asking deeper questions by giving them as many opportunities to do so as I could. This was done in verbal discussions, in writing, and, eventually, online, through a service called Edmodo.

Edmodo became my choice of social media because it was designed specifically for educators and students, and met all of my criteria. It looks similar to other social networking sites, but provides a safe place (password-protected and specific to each teacher who uses it) for teachers to extend the learning. On Edmodo, I posted examples of sophisticated discussion questions. As we

Type of Question	Guiding Verbs	Number of Questions Teacher Asked	Examples	Number of Questions Student Asked	Examples
Remembering: Can the student recall or remember the information?	Define, duplicate, list, memorize, recall, repeat, reproduce, state				
Understanding: Can the student explain ideas or concepts?	Classify, describe, discuss, explain, identify, locate, recognize, report, select, translate, paraphrase				
Applying: Can the student use the information in a new way?	Choose, demonstrate, dramatize, employ, illustrate, interpret, operate, schedule, sketch, solve, use, write				
Analyzing: Can the student distinguish between the different parts?	Appraise, compare, contrast, criticize, differentiate, discriminate, distinguish, examine, experiment, question, test				
Evaluating: Can the student justify a stand or decision?	Appraise, argue, defend, judge, select, support, value, evaluate				
Creating: Can the student create a new product or point of view?	Assemble, construct, create, design, develop, formulate, write				

Figure 3.2 Collection grid for questions/comments during book club discussions

moved through the project, I began to scaffold the discussion skills by starting the ideas and letting the kids ask the questions. From there, I would provide feedback to the students, giving them suggestions for improvement or giving them probing questions that would push them to the next level.

I spent time explicitly teaching my students about the question types. I wanted them to understand how different types of questions elicited different types of responses. I taught them the differences of inquiry, clarifying, critical thinking, and inference questioning. We discussed how the critical thinking and inference questioning developed their understanding more deeply and kept the dialogue going.

Increased results in student performance are important, and getting students talking to their parents about books was also extremely beneficial, but just as importantly, I began to see results in my own teaching techniques. I found that I was more effectively able to model good discussion questions, demonstrating exactly what I wanted in the book club and then transferring that approach into my World Cultures and Language Arts classes. As my skills on teaching depth increased, my leadership role in discussions decreased.

I definitely saw improvements on the types of questions asked by the students settling comfortably in the areas of analysis and evaluation versus the remembering and understanding types of questions that they were asking at the beginning of the project. The group definitely moved from being participants in the discussions to becoming the leaders of those discussions.

Keep the Conversation Going

I've come to enjoy the place where my book club has settled into. I have students who are motivated and interested in being there, we've found ways to bring ourselves up with the times using digital writing, and we've brought the level of discussion and writing to a sophisticated level that incorporates deep levels of thinking. Yet, I'm finding myself wondering how I can improve on what we've done. One aspect that would make this group more effective would be to continually draw in new group members.

A sense of community has been built, yet, we're leaving out some of the most important people from the school and community—the rest of the grade levels in our school and members of the towns in which we live. What would happen to the club if we included additional members of the school and outlying communities, and encouraged collaboration in a book discussion? I think perhaps it would help bridge some very important relationships that could only enhance the educational experience our students have and deepen our discussions.

I am dreaming of a project in which the club could choose a book and then encourage other students in grades 9–12 to join us in reading and discussing it. I dream of a club where there are more faculty members involved becoming part of the discussion. Likewise, I am dreaming of a club that extends the school walls, and bridges the discussion with the communities that contribute students to our building in getting them involved, as well. Our school is literally located in the middle of a rural area juxtaposed between two very small towns; we also are comprised of outlying communities 12 miles to the west and 20 miles to the east. Since no one town calls us their own, we really have some room to grow in the area of building a school-wide community base. What better way to build this than to invite the members of those towns to join us in a book club discussion?

What They Said

The first step I took was to make sure I told the students what I was looking for—I needed them to take ownership of the discussion, but I didn't expect them to do this immediately. I explained that I was going to teach them how to ask questions. I first modeled good discussion questions during the early meetings we held. On Edmodo, I wrote discussion questions that modeled what I was looking for (Figure 3.3). When we met at the following meeting, I pointed out how these questions gave the group more to discuss, rather than just short responses.

To help model good uses of discussion questions, I used pre-written questions from *The Hunger Games* I found online through the Almanace County Public Libraries, and chose the discussion questions that would evoke the most responses. There is no shame in using pre-written materials, as long as you have evaluated them and found them to be of good quality, and are not just using them in place of creating original ones or (gulp!) because you, yourself, haven't read the book at hand.

When I asked a question, we evaluated the amount of eagerness the students had in responding. We compared the questions against each other so we could determine what made the questions that elicited the most responses better than those that did not. For example, the question that encouraged the students to talk the most was, "Do you think Katniss and Peeta are the same people at the end of the games as they were when they stepped into the arena? How have they changed?" Each of the students in attendance offered their opinion without being called on. They offered opinions that were well-supported from the text and became very animated with their responses. When we finished the question, I asked them to look at how their demeanor changed completely when that question came up versus the previous discussion questions we had addressed. The students quickly noted the difference and thoughtfully considered why this

Shelby G. to ■ "'Williamson Book Club'"

something i'd like to comment on.. how books can lead to amazing conversations, bring together people and bring back memories (good or bad or sad depending). its just impressive. and how they can make you thunk about things. its phenominal. books are forever. we owe our lives to all those amazing, abstra authors out there!

☺ ✓ 2 Reactions · ○ 13 Replies · ⌇ Share   May 12, 2

Me · May 30, 2013
So, what is a book that has done this for you?
For me, it was Bridge to Terrabithia
Picture it. I was in 7th grade. One of my best friends rode the same bus to school as I did. We sat together every day. We had the best of times on that bus. The hours we spent. One day, I saw the ambulance go screeching by my house. As was my custom (and still is), I prayed for the people being affected by the ambulance and the medical personnel helping them. The next morning, I got on the bus, looked around, but I couldn't find Nicole. As the bus pulled away from my stop, I asked her neighbor where she was. She told me, "She's brain dead." What!? As I got to school, I learned she was hit by a car riding her bike the night before and she was in the ICU at Geisinger. At lunch time that day, I felt her spirit leave the earth. Can't explain it, but I knew she was gone. I plopped my head on the cafeteria table and sobbed. It was later that afternoon we got word that indeed she had died 12:20 pm. The precise moment I felt her leave. I don't know why I felt that, but I can tell you, I did.

Honestly? When they told me they were moving me to teach 7th grade, I cried. I didn't want to teach 7th grade. All I could remember was my 7th grade year when I lost my best friend, my grandmother, and my great grandfather all in the same year. In between that were all of those tragic friend moments (you know, the ones where your BFF won't talk to you anymore and has everyone else hating you for a reason you can't even begin to understand?). hormones, sadness, happiness, and friendships that are the best ever.
So, a little peek into Mrs. Morral's life. Your life will never be same, will it? ;) lless.

 Shelby G. · May 31, 2013
no. and books where someone you love leaves i can totally and utterly connect to. kadin's leaving and i might not ever see him again. kota is moving up to highschool. alot of people are leaving, but. instead of dwelling upon their departure, i have to enjoy the time i have with them <3

 Jailin B. · Jun 4, 2013
mines try not to breathe..uhm yeah. that book was great. i um yeah i had alot to connect with in that book...thanks to zach nick trey n shelb though..not as much as i could have. which is VERY good.

 Shelby G. · · Jun 5, 2013
yea. mine is probably _____ black beauty. a favorite from when I was 6. ive read it at least twice every year since..thats alottt and I never read books over. it connects me with my love of animals, my horses (that are gone) and having friends that leave. and the cruelty of life. but how there is always a light at the tunnel. its all about the future, right jai? I don't feel like repeating that rant again. although it WAS quite inspirational, I think.

Figure 3.3 Edmodo screen shot

was so. They identified that this question was not a yes/no question and that it required them to give their own opinions and support their answer.

The immediate result of my efforts was livelier discussions for my book club. Following these methods led to deeper meaning in reading the texts and increased motivation, engagement, and ownership in my students. Their discussions were occurring more frequently. I started observing students having conversations about the books they read with each other in the hallway between classes, at their lockers, and passing by the teachers in the hallway. Because the students were conversing about the books in public places, their excitement grew. I began having students ask if they could join the book club so they could read the books that the kids were discussing. And book club members shared that they had their parents, siblings, and best friends read the books, as well. One book in particular, *Life on the Refrigerator Door,* sparked a lot of this type of discussion. A story about a teen girl who was figuring out her relationship with her single-parent mother who was working long hours, the two were reduced to communicating through notes left on the refrigerator door. Parents and students alike found deep connections in the words and emotions that spilled from the pages (Figure 3.4).

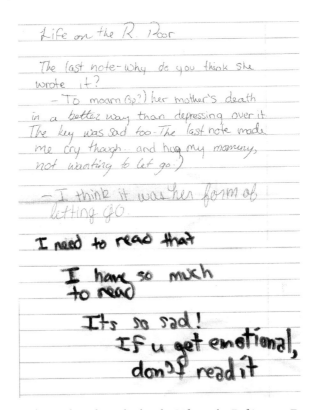

Figure 3.4 Note exchange based on the book, *Life on the Refrigerator Door*

Students began to evaluate the books on multiple levels. One of the writing activities that sparked the most examples of sophisticated discussion was a note-writing session. I invited them to write notes to one another while they were in the book club. This activity appealed to these kids at the heart of their world: in middle school right in the midst of the importance of social activity. From the samples I collected (see Figure 3.5 and 3.6), I found several of them to be very intriguing.

Students were writing with emotion and their typical passionate interactions screamed out loud through their pass-the-note activity. If I were to venture on a reason for the passionate writing, I'd have to say that this activity hit them right where they are as social beings—concerned about each other's thoughts. Writing notes allowed their voices to be heard loud and clear, and their writing mimicked their real-life social talk. This was something that had been a rare occurrence in the early days of the book club.

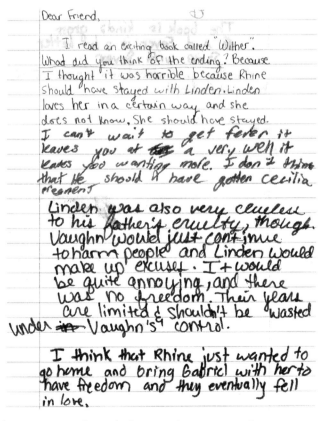

Figure 3.5 Students converse through the pass-the-note exercise

Melissa Morral

Figure 3.6 Student voices are evident in the pass-the-note exercise

In Figure 3.7, the chart shows the natural progression of sample questions and comments for various book club meetings. As we progressed throughout the year, the students started moving away from the superficial and into sophisticated questions and comments on a regular basis. A shift had definitely taken place.

Perhaps one of the biggest challenges a teacher has in getting students to read is providing them with ample copies of books that are current and appealing. Frequent purchases have to occur to keep the list up-to-date, but this can be costly to either the teacher running the program or the district supporting that teacher. To begin the project, I was able to find funding through our local Endless Mountains Writing Project, and then was able to supplement that through Donors Choose (*www.donorschoose.org*). Donors Choose is a non-profit program that provides teachers ability way to request materials needed for a classroom project. Teachers post project ideas on the website for which

Superficial Question/Comments	Sophisticated Questions/Comments
It was a really good book.	I think the book showed how important friendships are through dogs.
I want the second book.	Would it have had the same impact with humans?
I find the book better than the movie.	This book reminded me of Shelby's horses and their separation anxiety.
What was your favorite part of the book?	I'm reminded of the very close friendship I have with my friend Leah.
Who was your favorite character?	I think the mom shouldn't have told the authorities. If she had tried to help him, then Cole wouldn't have gotten in so much trouble.
What were the boys doing when they put up the ghost?	This is why I think it would have been better for Cole.
Who was your favorite demigod of the seven?	Extension: discussion of Touching Spirit Bear lead to a deep discussion on addictions and how they impact the various people in the lives of the addict.
	What faction do you think you would have been in?
	Why do you think Caleb would let Tris die?
	Ruthless people would be drawn to Dauntless. You have to want to try just about anything to be in that faction.
	Calm and peaceful people probably would go toward Amity. They want nothing but peace between the factions.
	Candor are brutally honest! You say whatever is on your mind. Lying is not an option. Not sure I'd like to be in that faction if I didn't want to hear the truth.
	What part of the book took a turn that you were not expecting?
	Why do you think Joey and Rusty mixed their blood to seal the deal forever?
	If you were Rusty and you made the blood pacts would you do all of the things Joey did just to go along?

Figure 3.7 Samples of superficial vs. sophisticated discussion questions and comments

they need funding, and donors from around the world browse the posted projects and help fund projects at their choosing.

Through this program alone, my book club for the 2012–2013 school year was able to purchase 22 current titles (total of 85 books) for just under $900 through Donors Choose, all provided by kind donors who saw a need and helped financially. Purchasing this number of books would not have been possible if Donors Choose had not been available.

Book Club Titles Read for 2012–2013 School Year
Titles purchased with funds from Endless Mountain Writing Project, Donors Choose, or school district funds

---

A Monster Calls by Patrick Ness
Divergent by Veronica Roth
Enclave by Ann Aguirre
The Fault in Our Stars by John Green
Fever by Lauren DeStefano
Glass by Ellen Hopkins
Heart to Heart by Lurlene McDaniel
Here, There Be Dragons by James A. Owen
Icefall by Matthew J. Kirby
Insurgent by Veronica Roth
Interview with a Vampire by Anne Rice
Island's End by Padma Venkatraman
Legend by Marie Lu
Life on the Refrigerator Door by Alice Kuipers
Lost Hero by Rick Roirdan
Mark of Athena by Rick Roirdan
Nightjohn by Gary Paulsen
Outpost by Ann Aguirre
Princess Academy by Shannon Hale
Sever by Lauren DeStefano
Son of Poseidon by Rick Roirdan
The Space Between by Brenna Yovanoff
Starters by Lissa Price
Stolen by Lucy Christopher
Swear to Howdy by Wendelin Van Draanen
Touching Spirit Bear by Ben Mikaelsen
Vampire Rising by Alex VanHelsing
The Vampire Stalker by Allison Van Deupeir
Voice of the Undead by Alex VanHelsing
The Wave by Todd Strasser
What My Mother Doesn't Know by Sonya Sones
Where the Red Fern Grows by Wilson Rawls
The Winter Room by Gary Paulsen
Wither by Lauren DeStefano

Figure 3.8 List of titles purchased for the 2012–2013 school year for my book club

Something to Talk About

A book club like this one can be replicated. What it takes is a teacher who sees the value of writing and reading (discussing) books and wants to see results. This could happen in the classroom, as well, instead of during personal time.

Thinking about getting started can be daunting. What you need to do first is find out if there is interest. The students who are enthusiastic about this type of group are going to get the fire going under all of the other students who will attend. Allowing for student choice is an important piece. If students hold the ownership to what they are reading, they are more likely going to discuss what they read, and ownership will lead to deeper thinking, thus, deeper discussions.

As you can imagine, coming up with funds can be discouraging, as well, but using an organization such as Donors Choose can help. Once funds are secure, and students have selected titles to read, it will be important to organize time and place. Flexibility might be necessary for both the teacher advising such a group and the students who are participating. At this level, students are involved in all kinds of activities that might interfere. Likewise, a full teaching schedule can impede the success of finding the perfect time.

Have fun. It might be cliché to say, but if you and the students aren't having fun, the work becomes overwhelming and successful deep discussions cannot happen. Read what they are reading. Find passion in reading it. If you love it, let that shine through. Don't be afraid to discuss a book with the kids in the hallway as they pass by on their way to their next classes. And likewise, if you dislike a book, do so with passion. Don't be afraid to show your true feelings about it, but don't miss the opportunity to discuss why it was so displeasing to you. Face it—as adults, I'm sure we all run across books that we don't care for. We might abandon them. We may never finish them. That's ok. That is what real readers do, but there is often a lot of forethought that goes into leaving the text in the dust.

Seek a community of readers. Get your colleagues to join you. Be role models for your students. Let them see you reading and discussing, and allow them to join in, as well. Have teachers from the content areas join you on a book or two and be part of the discussion. Not only will it encourage your colleagues to grow in their reading repertoire, but they will be more examples for students to follow.

References

Barry, C. (2010). From great texts—to great thinking. *Educational Leadership, 67*(6), 42–46.

Cochran, D. (2007). The new Bloom's. *The Creative Educator, 1*(2), 14–16.

Gallagher, K. (2004). *Deeper reading: Comprehending challenging texts.* Portland, ME: Stenhouse Publishers.

Gambrell, L. (2011). Seven rules of engagement: What's most important to know about motivation to read. *The Reading Teacher, 65*(3), 172–178.

Hathaway, L. (2011, October 7). How to use virtual book clubs to engage students in reading. *Eye On Education.* Retrieved from www.routledge.com/eyeoneducation/blog/1306/

Kinser, R. (2011, September 20). Virtual book clubs: Connecting adolescent readers. *Education Week Teacher: Teacher Leaders Network.* Retrieved from www.edweek.org/tm/articles/2011/09/20/kinser_virtual.html

McGaha, J. M., & Igo, B. (2012). Assessing high school students' reading motivation in a voluntary summer reading program. *Journal of Adolescent and Adult Literacy, 55*(5), 417–427.

Richetti, C., & Sheerin, J. (1999). Helping students ask the right questions. *Educational Leadership: The Constructivist Classroom. ASCD.* Retrieved from www.ascd.org/publications/educational-leadership/nov99/vol57/num03/Helping-Students-Ask-the-Right-Questions.aspx

Rothstein, D., & Santana, L. (2011). Teaching students to ask their own questions. *Harvard Education Letter, 27*(5). Retrieved from http://hepg.org/hel/article/507

Scharber, C. (2009). Digital literacies: Online book clubs. *Journal of Adolescent and Adult Literacy, 52*(5), 433–437.

Silver, H. F., Dewing, R. T., & Perini, M. J. (2012). *The core six: Essential strategies for achieving excellence with the common core.* Alexandria, VA: ASCD.

Spencer, J. T. (2011). 10 ways to help students ask better questions. *TeachPaperless.* Retrieved from http://teachpaperless.blogspot.com/2011/04/10-ways-to-help-students-ask-better.html

Sweeny, S. M. (2010). Writing for the instant messaging and text messaging generation: Using new literacies to support writing instruction. *Journal of Adolescent and Adult Literacy, 54*(2), 121–130.

CHAPTER

Writing Connections
The Not-So-Secret Mission of Parental Involvement
Bobbi Button

Future Agent

I feverishly wrote for Mrs. Comfort first using a notebook, then an old Mac that printed on dot matrix paper (the kind with a series of small holes used for grasping the edges as it printed onto a roll of mint green and white paper). She encouraged my stories and often spattered my pages with brief comments like, "Words cannot express the power of this story" and "I cannot wait to see where you end." That was journalism class my sophomore year and creative writing class my junior year. She not only created a safe place for me to write about unwavering high school love and my crappy home life, but she fostered a passion for the written word that ultimately led me to become editor of the school newspaper my senior year and an English teacher years later. I wanted to be just like her.

What Mrs. Comfort didn't do was mark every single spelling or grammar mistake. She didn't critique the mechanics as much as she did the material. She wasn't afraid to assign a story that she knew would keep my brain buzzing with ideas and images for days. Oh, she didn't ignore the comma splices or the fragments, but they were never the main focus. Today, looking back at some of those early writings, I see many unnoted mistakes. They weren't overlooked. She knew what she was doing. She was showing me the passion that drives good writers. My students needed to experience that passion.

The Mission

Writing is fundamental in the mission of raising literate children. Students need to see the good side of writing. They need to know that it is ok to enjoy the job of writing an assignment. Parents need to know that focusing too much on spelling and grammar mistakes can hinder this enjoyment and make students apprehensive about writing. Postlehwaite and Ross (1992) "found that parental involvement in all its various forms, when initiated by schools and teachers, was the single best predictor of student achievement in reading for grades 2 and 8" (in Rasinski, Padak, & Pytash, 2009, p. 94). We already know that there is a relationship between the frequency with which students write and how much their writing improves. This just makes sense—you don't get better at something if you don't actually *do* that something! It became my mission to supplement my classroom approach with this, with parental involvement, so my students would get support and quality writing experiences both at school and at home.

Connecting a reluctant child with the love of writing isn't an easy task for any educator. Connecting their reluctant parents with the love of writing can be even more daunting! "Parents often recognize the importance of playing an active role in their child's early years of schooling but fail to appreciate fully the need for positive involvement supporting educational growth in the middle and high school years" (Rasinski, Padak, & Pytash, 2009, p. 93). This chapter is designed to share the tips and tricks I used to ignite the fever for writing in students and parents and to help them understand how writing has changed in perception and practice in the 21st century. The chapter is, in a way, a means of paying back Mrs. Comfort for her inspiration and support as I have developed as a writer and teacher.

My mission for the school year focused on helping the parents of my seventh and eighth grade students to better connect with their children's writing, understand its purpose and place within the classroom, and to open them to the idea of actually enjoying the task. My small, rural Pennsylvania school district prides itself on strong test scores and equally strong sports statistics. It sits among majestic mountains and expects teachers to produce students of equal strength and beauty. Yet, the idea of writing for practice or pleasure isn't common, encouraged, or expected. Like students, parents focus on the red marks more than the remarks.

Mission Critical

For many, red ink indicates effort toward creating spellers and grammarians. For some, correct spelling and grammar equates to students who are better prepared for their future. When the enjoyable side of writing appears, it's not understood to be a valuable asset. Michelle Cox, Christina Ortmeier-Hooper, and Katherine Tirabassi (2009), authors of "Teaching Writing for the Real World," say, "often we hear complaints about how their academic classes and the writing they do in English class don't seem relevant in the 'real world' of work" (p. 73). Their article outlines a community-based writing project, and it inspired me to move forward with this initiative. I wanted to create a community within the confines of my classroom where parents and students could write together and enjoy it.

Lynda Wade Sentz, author of *Write with Me* (2011), shares the staggering statistic that "only 30% of parents of school-age children and only 27% of educators write for enjoyment" (p. 33). She goes on to say what I feel is the crux for my project: "school-age children potentially are at risk for not having adequate writing role models in their lives" (p. 33). Of course, there are many separating factors between generations. However, one fact remains steadfast: "communication and discussions among parents, teachers, and students have continually been found to raise student achievement" (Rasinski, Padak, & Pytash, 2009, p. 94). Once students realize that the people they spend the majority of their school-aged life with—parents and teachers—are on the same page, they know that achievement is expected and will be monitored more so than they thought.

Another one of the separating factors in the writing of today's students is technology. Student writing and reading is different because the technology available at school isn't the same as what's available at home. I needed to make a connection between the academic literacies and home literacies before I could suggest anything as radical as writing together.

The National Council of Teachers of English (2009) reports that educators "recognize that out-of-school literacy practices are as critical to students' development as what occurs in the classroom" (p. 1). In addition to linking parents' and students' literacies, I needed to find a way to share the updated practices of teaching writing. I needed them to see that just because they didn't have a teacher like Mrs. Comfort, didn't mean they were any less of a writer.

When a parent sees a mistake in spelling or grammar that is not marked in the almighty red ink of the teacher, they instantly feel the teacher has short-changed the student. As Anne Wescott Dodd (2012) points out in her article, "What Do Parents Mean When They Talk about Writing 'Basics' and What Should English Teachers Do about It?" many parents are unaware of modern-day teaching practices (p. 58). Too often, our teaching responsibilities focus on the students and we forget about the power of the parents to impact student learning. When we don't reach out to parents, they are left to filter their child's school life through their own experience as a student. Changes in pedagogy really need to be shared with our families and communities.

Dodd's article corroborates with my thought that parents need to understand the way writing is being taught and how it will improve literacy. Parents need to understand why students are not being graded the way they were, or thought they were, years ago. They need be familiar with educational jargon and buzzwords like "21st century literacies," "Common Core State Standards," "rubrics," "writing across the curriculum," and the multitude of other practices being used by "highly qualified" teachers.

When this brainchild started to develop, I was more than excited. I wanted every single student to love writing. I planned four evenings in the fall of 2012 that would touch on writing for the love of the art, and explain how it is taught now compared to the way parents were taught, how it helps develop productive members of society, and the way technology in the 21st century has changed it. I wanted parents and students to know that what is being taught is based on a prescribed set of standards designed "to help ensure that students gain adequate mastery of a range of skills and application" (Common Core State Standard Initiative, 2010, p. 42).

"Write with Your Child" evenings were placed on the calendar in the school office. I was nervous because I wasn't the writing teacher. I thought the students had a disadvantage because they didn't get to experience my passion for the love of writing. However, there were many things I knew for certain. I knew that parental involvement would enhance the learning. I had the blessing of my principal, which is crucial under any circumstance. I knew that not everyone had experience with 21st-century learning in our rural area, so that would be something to use to draw them to the class. I knew that using brightly colored flyers is how I would advertise. I introduced my nights in each of my eighth grade classes and my single seventh grade class, while I implored my colleagues to do the same. I knew I could inspire parents once I got them to my classroom. I was passionate.

Mission Possible

I created prompt papers, typed up a post-evening survey, gathered notebooks and pens, and bought cookies, candy, and juice. I even made arrangements with the culinary teacher to provide refreshments for future evenings. I created a buffet line and a writing circle in my classroom. Then, I waited. And waited. Nobody showed. I cried. Discouraged and deflated, I wanted an explanation.

Swarms of thoughts blurred my vision and I ignored the whispers in my mind that suggested parents didn't like to write, students didn't like to write, and maybe this was a horrible idea. I also ignored the more realistic whispers that suggested I wasn't passionate enough and maybe the flyer didn't make it home. I talked with my principal, professor, and colleagues, but it was my husband, the dairy farmer, who gave me the answer when I had just decided

How important is writing in the world outside of school?	Very important	82%
	Somewhat important	18%
	Not important	0%
Do you consider your child's writing ability an important part of his/her education?	Very important	92%
	Somewhat important	8%
	Not important	0%
Do you assist your child in writing assignments?	Always	10%
	Sometimes	83%
	Never	7%
Would you be willing to attend "Write with Your Child" evenings?	Yes	48%
	Maybe	39%
	Never	13%
How would you rate your writing ability?	High	37%
	Mediocre	62%
	Low	1%

Figure 4.1 Results from a parent survey about writing and writing workshops

to give up. "Can't you talk to parents about writing at conference time?" Sometimes, all I need is the obvious thrown into my face.

For conference meetings, I created a survey addressing the questions surrounding writing and my "Write with your Child" evenings (see Figure 4.1). I needed to figure out why nobody wanted to write. Each parent was asked to fill out one survey at student-led conferences in November. Although I'm certain that some of the questions would be answered differently if they had not been answered in school, I took the 48% of responses that answered 'yes' to "Would you be willing to attend 'Write with Your Child' evenings" as a sign that I could not yet give up!

I retooled and created a new plan, deciding that the "Write with Your Child" evenings was a mission I would once again accept.

Now that I knew that the issue was not one of parent interest or that they didn't value writing, I decided I would need to step up the advertising campaign and really get the word out. The first night was advertised using a community service bulletin board broadcast on a local radio station. This service was free and all it took to get it going was a quick call to the radio station, followed by an email about the program. Five to ten minutes of effort and the word went out to the entire listening audience!

Next, I used a service that our district already had in place to communicate with parents: *Parent Link*. This service sent another wave of notice in the form of a phone call from my principal that went out to all parents. Next, I designed an eye-catching flyer for the program, which the local branch of the National Writing Project (see Figure 4.2) printed in full color. These went home stapled

Writing:

It's behind every jingle, movie, text, and Tweet. How should *your* child be learning to *use* it to get ahead?

For an answer....join Mrs. Button for "Williamson Write Nights"!

Free sessions offered to help you keep tabs on how your child's education and future is changing.

Please let us know if you plan to attend so that we can plan supplies and refreshments!

- Why was this <u>writing</u> assignment graded this way?
- How can <u>writing</u> skills be used in a job or career?
- What is the Common Core and how will it change how students are asked to read, write, and think?
- Technology: a tool that helps people <u>write</u> and think, or a time-waster?

Room J130 Williamson Middle School   <u>Bring your child!</u>
January 31, February 7, February 21 6:00-8:00PM

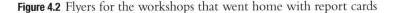

Figure 4.2 Flyers for the workshops that went home with report cards

to each report card. Last, I put a sign in front of our school announcing the dates each evening would take place.

All of this ammunition worked—they showed up! A short survey at the end of the first evening seemed to say all I needed to hear. When asked to "describe your family's attitude towards writing," one person wrote "*possible.*" Well, that was all the affirmation I needed. Based on the goose bumps prickling my arm as I read that, I thought it wouldn't matter if nobody showed up to the remaining two evenings. I had accomplished something. I had hooked them! From there on out, goose bumps, smiles, and amazing ideas sprouted from these evenings.

Discussions about the Common Core Standards, grading, and technology were some of the other highlights of these evenings. I loosely defined the Common Core State Standards (CCSS) as follows:

- They are the best practices and represent a national effort to give a common understanding of what students are expected to learn in English language arts (ELA) and math.
- July 2010—PA became the 18th state to adopt them.
- July 2013—The transition from our current standards will be fully implemented.(Our state department originally set this as a target date.)

Based on the feedback I got at our sessions, I realized that parents and guardians had no idea that such changes were coming, but they were sincerely interested and happy to be let into the information loop. I also referred them to the website for the Pennsylvania Department of Education, and I could see from their facial expressions that it had never really occurred to them that this website was there for parents, as well. They assumed only educators could peruse, investigate, and use the information. It was their turn to have the obvious-in-your-face moment! And, wow, what a conversation followed. We discussed the difference between the testing practice of the state prior to CCSS and after. We ended the CCSS section with parents and students writing about the practice. It was refreshing to hear that they not only supported the idea, but were intent on understanding the framework.

I used a PowerPoint demonstration to segue into the use of technology, which then led to another discussion about modern-day methods of grading writing. Parents had very little familiarity with rubrics up to that point. Well, some of them had *heard* of them. I shared with them the rubric that my state adopted using the state's department of education website, www.pde.state.pa.us.

This was the place in the evening when I got to explain the difference between conventions and style. I showed them the reason why each comma splice or spelling mistake is not marked the first time. They now understood that, eventually, their child would be graded on each component of the writing rubric, but, without a doubt, creating a love of writing was the ultimate goal. And although the parents agreed that not everyone will be a passionate writer, the best part of the evening was the writing we did together.

Not only did parents learn something, everyone in the room was touched by the stories we shared. Some professionals would scoffingly call this part "fluff," or joke about "warm fuzzies." I call it an ingredient of great writing. This was where the group connected as people. Some of my favorites included one from a grandmother who once drove a hazardous waste truck for a living, and another from a mom who works at a welcome center along a major highway, not to mention the imagery from a parent who has published poetry in "real hard cover books."

The second evening I walked parents and students through a mini writing assignment, following the steps of the writing process. Students were almost shocked that I was teaching their parents something they had been practicing for years, but parents were unaware that this process, like all others used in my classroom, is researched based. According to Pressley, Mohan, Fingeret, Reffitt, and Raphael-Bogaert (2007), "when students are taught to plan, draft, and revise in a self-regulated fashion, their writing improves a great deal" (p. 24). All of the students agreed that although following the writing process wasn't always easy, it made for a better finished product. This discussion was a great setup for the evening's guest speaker, community member Michael Vayansky. He was asked to speak about writing as it related to the real world. I had several reasons for inviting him to speak. He not only works in one of the more well-known local factories as an engineer, but he is also a school board member and the husband of an English teacher. His opening question to the kids was "You write because you want to?" It made more than one of us giggle. Michael explained how writing is used from the time a person walks into the factory until the product is shipped out. He explained why it is important to know your audience and your task. The accomplishment with his visit was the impression on the students that writing is a real world job skill and vital to becoming a successful member of society.

The final meeting was such an inspiring evening. Students told the adults their favorite ways to write. The week before, I had attendees create their own writing prompt on a sticky note before leaving. I typed the prompts up in varying fonts on a sheet of brightly colored paper and added the title, "What were we thinking?" (see Figure 4.3). We wrote using these prompts and then shared our work out loud. We used picture prompts because Troy, who was the youngest of several brothers being raised by his grandmother, had remembered a quick write I did earlier in the year using a picture of a llama. He loved it.

> ### What were we thinking?
>
> **What would it be like to live in a fairytale and what would you do?**
>
> Give your thoughts on gun control and school safety.
>
> **Write about a time you were given an important responsibility.**
>
> Do you have a pet? Write a funny or sad pet story.
>
> **You're sledding and the only thing to stop you from sliding into a major highway is a stone wall. Write about what's going through your head.**
>
> What is your favorite food? What is your least favorite food? Write about a time you experienced one or both.
>
> **You're locked in a bathroom with no electronics, no books, nothing. How would you occupy the time?**
>
> Write about a serious time in your life using nothing but facts. Don't include feelings or thoughts.
>
> **Have you ever panicked because you cannot find something for work or school and then discovered it was right in front of you?**
>
> You are going on a trip. Your travel companions warn you to pack light. However, you over-pack. Describe the scene of you loading your luggage and then unpacking it.
>
> **Describe a struggle or misfortune you've encountered at work or in the classroom and how it changed you.**
>
> What song makes you want to jump up and move? Why? When is the first time you recall hearing it? Do you know the words?

Figure 4.3 Student- and parent-created writing prompts

Troy does not normally write at all. The llama was ugly, but caused an explosion of writing ideas.

Our discussion moved to the multitasking students of the 21st century, who can listen to music, write, and have a TV on at the same time. We discussed how some learn best one way and others learn best another, and why it's important to not only know which way you learn best, but why and how. We practiced listening to music while writing (I chose from three genres: rock, country, and classical), and having a totally silent room. We demonstrated a talk-and-type app on an iPad, which was foreign to most parents. They were interested, engaged. They were becoming passionate. My end-of-the-evening survey (see Figure 4.4) would prove that, since we first met in January, my project had exploded in a good way.

Last Evening Survey

Name _____

Student Name _____

Is this your first time attending a Write with Your Child Evening?   Yes   No

If yes, why **didn't** you attend the previous two? _____

If no, why **did** you attend these events? _____

Do you think the information shared during these three nights was valuable?

Yes   No

Why or why not? _____

_____

_____

_____

_____

Please tell me one thing you liked about this evening and one area you think
I could improve.

_____

_____

_____

_____

Would you attend if there is a series of writing evenings in the spring?

Yes   No

Thank you for taking the time from your busy schedules to share my love
of writing. I hope this not only helps you understand the writing world of
your child, but I hope it inspires you both to write.

Figure 4.4 Last evening survey

Next Step: More Missions!

It wasn't very long ago that my innards were wrenching with disappointment when nobody attended my first scheduled evening in the fall. I had sunk. I was done. Blah, blah, blah! I'm glad I didn't give up. With some coaching from colleagues and directors, I gave it another shot. It's pretty phenomenal what happened. Parents and students really came together, and we had meaningful dialogue and bonded on many levels. I think I learned as much from them as they did from talking with me and each other. Mission possible. Mission completed.

But then, I was behind my desk gathering papers and getting ready for class when Ian approached, "Mrs. Button, I can't make it to those Write Night things because of basketball practice, but I think you should have a creative writing club during school because I like to write and I've got a lot of good stories to tell." Now, my big mouth houses a pretty big smile 90% of the time, but after this comment, it doubled, no, tripled in size. Before I could say, "I have too much to do," I was getting the blessing of my principal and Ian was hand writing CWC (Creating Writing Club) posters announcing the weekly meetings that are now taking place in my classroom every Friday. The spark in Ian wasn't the only amazing thing that started with these evenings.

Another student had attended with her mother, who not only happens to be the art teacher, but a fellow EMWP teacher consultant. After the sessions, I received a jammed-packed-with-ideas email from her, and we are planning to partner up and offer a new evening series combining art and writing for students and parents. Making journals and artist trading cards—these are the projects that have my creative innards doing summersaults.

Next Mission

Parents need to be involved in order to understand what is going on in their child's school and classrooms. If they understand, they can be your biggest advocates. Epstein and Dauber (1991) state that "parental interaction with children's education at home increases when teachers make parental involvement a component of their teaching practice, regardless of the child's age or grade level" (in Rasinski, Padak, & Pytash, 2009, p. 95). With funding cuts, high-stakes testing, and the emphasis on literacy, it won't hurt to have extra cheerleaders. So, talk to the ELA and Reading teachers in your school to discuss how you can implement Write with Your Child nights. If you're not comfortable taking on the task yourself, team up with another educator in your building or district. If you still cannot find the extra help, contact your local National Writing Project chapter and they will direct you to teachers who are excited to help. After you have brainstormed, set up an appointment with your principal.

At the meeting, discuss not only what Write with Your Child nights are and why you want to host these evenings, but be sure to talk about the number of nights, advertising, funding, and research. Perhaps offering to discuss the outcomes with your school board will be all you need to acquire permission. Be sure to mention all of the free resources you have within your community. Perhaps you don't need to meet at school, but can host a night at the local YMCA or community center. Advertising can be a public service broadcast on TV and radio, as well as the daily announcements at school. Not to mention, you may be able to place an ad in the school paper or local paper.

Regardless of where you host the events, make sure the focus is not only to share the importance of writing, but to ignite the passion of your subject. "A family-school partnership is strengthened by the positive acknowledgement of family contributions to students' literacy practices" (Rasinski, Padak, & Pytash, 2009, p. 99). There are a gigantic number of articles and books written for educators praising the involvement of parents. Read them. Share them with your administrators and coworkers. You may be surprised with how doing so rekindles your passion in education. There is no reason writing cannot spark a passion in every subject area. From explaining the steps to solving an equation in math, to using imagery to describe the outcome of a hypothesis in science, you will smile when you read the thoughts of your students. Okay, you may also cry, but in that case, you have the chance to elaborate, explain, or redirect. Or, in other words, you will have a chance to really teach.

References

Common Core State Standard Initiative. (2010). *Common Core State Standards for English Language Arts & Literacy in History/Social Studies, Science, and Technical Subjects.* Retrieved from www.corestandards.org/

Cox, M., Ortmeier-Hooper, C., & Tirabassi, K. E. (2009). Teaching writing for the "real world": Community and workplace writing. *English Journal, 98*(5), 72–80.

Dodd, A. W. (2012). What do parents mean when they talk about writing "basics" and what should English teachers do about it? *English Journal, 85*(1), 58–61.

National Council of Teachers of English. (2009). *Writing between the lines—and everywhere else: A report from NCTE.* Retrieved from www.ncte.org/library/NCTEFiles/Press/WritingbetweentheLinesFinal.pdf

Pressley, M., Mohan L., Fingeret, L., Reffitt, K., & Raphael-Bogaert, L. (2007). What should a school do to teach students to write? In S. Graham, C. A. MacArthur, & J. Fitzgerald (Eds.), *Best practices in writing instruction* (pp. 13–27). New York, NY: Guilford Press.

Rasinski, T., Padak, N., & Pytash, K. (2009). Promoting adolescent literacy through parental involvement: Making it happen. In K. D. Wood & W. Blanton (Eds.), *Literacy instruction for adolescents* (pp. 92–106). New York, NY: Guilford Press.

Sentz, L. (2011). *Write with me.* Larchmont, NY: Eye on Education.

CHAPTER

5 Connecting the Curriculum
Some Book on Cambodia

Karin Knaus and Stacey Segur

Some Book on Cambodia

So, this chapter has two authors. Collectively, we've spent more than 25 years in the classroom, all of them teaching research. We actually *like* research. We're those nerds you see in the faculty room who get excited about getting started on a new project each year. And yet, we always know, it's going to be a struggle. We know that our kids *should* have a general sense of what research looks like and what credible resources are. We also know our kids *ought* to, by the time we see them as juniors and seniors, know that there's more to searching for information than just feeding topics into Google. But, *should* + *ought* do not = *do*. We came together to work on this project because we found ourselves each year sharing the same lament about doing research with older students: it's as if we're starting from scratch. We have to devote time to teaching about avoiding plagiarism, evaluating sources, organizing the Works Cited pages, and formatting, as if the students have never encountered these concepts before. John Keating (*Dead Poets Society*) never had to deal with this!

When our students learn research skills in one big chunk, it isn't surprising that they are overwhelmed and do less than their best on the finished products. Just recently, one of our colleagues received a Works Cited page from a middle school student that literally had listed as a citation: *Some Book on Cambodia*. No dates, no author, no sense of either MLA or APA format. It's easy to blame the student in situations like this, but, as teachers, we had to ask ourselves, are we setting kids up for this kind of failure?

Smoothing the Path

Knowing how to find answers to our daily questions and dilemmas is part of navigating modern life. Knowing where information comes from is part of evaluating its quality. Imagine how often we (and our students) use Google or Bing to find an answer to a real life or school-related question. Is it not important that we show kids how to find the best information, evaluate it, and use it, whether it is for a college-level research paper or in preparation to buy a first car?

The answer, of course, is a resounding "YES!" We questioned whether this one, monumental task was enough to create the foundation to retain and use these skills throughout students' future lives. We've all seen kids get their papers back and flip to the final page, interested only in their final grades. At the end of the day, the janitor makes extra dumpster trips because of all the immediately discarded papers. And with the papers goes the weeks of work on teaching how to do research. Is there a way to build a foundation that could last a lifetime? This is where we began.

Our study took place in two rural junior-senior high schools, grades 7–12, one consisting of 360 students and the other, 481 students.

Research about Research

First, we wondered about teachers in other content areas. We have seen our students working on projects in other disciplines, spending time on the Internet and in our libraries gathering information. If students had such limited knowledge and skill with doing research effectively in English class, where we teach it explicitly, were other teachers struggling, too? And was it possible that there were some teachers choosing not to require research because they weren't sure how to teach the necessary skills?

We started our project by gaining the permission and support of our administration; our building principals gave permission to survey our faculties during an in-service day at the beginning of the school year. Next, we created a survey of questions, keeping our own teaching dilemmas in mind, that would truly address what we wanted to investigate, such as the teachers' expectations of students' research skills and what teachers wished their students knew about research. We wanted to know who was "doing research" in our building. What were they expecting of our kids? What did they hope and wish our kids could do, and at what grade level? Then, we distributed these surveys to our high school (7th through 12th grades) faculty colleagues in all content areas. The surveys were anonymous and voluntary, but in both schools, the majority of teachers responded. The survey also included a section just for English language arts (ELA) teachers, as the responsibility for teaching these skills falls to them. Sixty-one faculty surveys were analyzed. Figure 5.1 shows the survey.

Research Skills Survey

As a part of our participation in the Endless Mountains Writing Project's Advanced Institute, we are performing research about how to teach students research skills. This includes how to choose a reasonable topic, efficiently finding sources, evaluating sources, appropriately citing information to avoid plagiarism, quoting and paraphrasing information from sources, and creating a bibliography in an approved format (we use MLA). Our ultimate goal is to design a creative and effective sequence for teaching research skills and building on them throughout students' school years so that they have a greater mastery of research by the time that they graduate.

Your participation is voluntary, but it represents the first step in our research about how to plan this sequence. This survey is anonymous.

Subject(s) I teach:

Grade level(s) I teach:

Do you require students to perform research in your class?

If yes, what task(s) do you ask them to do (ex: research a person and make a poster; research a topic and write a paper, etc.)? Please identify in what grade, if you teach more than one.

What research skills do you expect your students to have by the time that they reach your class (ex: efficiently find sources, evaluate sources for quality, use in-text citations, create a bibliography in an approved format, etc.)?

What research skills do you wish your students had?

Other comments about our students' research abilities:

IF YOU ARE A LANGUAGE ARTS TEACHER, PLEASE ALSO ANSWER THE FOLLOWING:

When teaching research, writing, and/or format, what are your strengths? What are your weaknesses? What is the most challenging part of teaching research?

When learning research, writing, and/or format, what are your students' strengths? What are their weaknesses? What is most challenging for them about any of these?

Please share any lesson/unit ideas that truly work for you when teaching research, writing, and/or format.

Figure 5.1 Survey for faculty regarding research skills

Faculty Practices and Perceptions

The results indicated that 65.6% of the faculty at our schools required research from students. Of that percentage, research-related tasks included researching people and/or events, and generating PowerPoint presentations, posters/flyers, and papers/essays. Many of the educators noted that they expected students to know the following: finding and evaluating multiple credible sources, citing, avoiding plagiarism, and creating a bibliography. Sixty-one percent of the teachers also responded that they wished that their students were able to apply these skills, and many of these teachers indicated that they felt students lacked efficient research skills and that plagiarism was common.

The majority of ELA teachers felt that they were strongest in emphasizing citations and being patient; however, many had weaknesses with communicating with students about citations, underestimating the amount of time that research takes, and finding worthwhile projects that students would want to do. This group felt that the challenges of teaching students about research include connecting these skills to the world, teaching citations, getting students to do quality work instead of being intimidated by it, and figuring out necessary skills that need to be taught at the middle-school levels. ELA teachers noted that the students' research strengths were organization, using outside information as support, locating sources on the Internet, and utilizing technology, while the students struggled with plagiarism, citing, evaluating sources, and formatting.

Once we compiled these results, we wanted to see how they compared to the larger body of professional research that was available from similar studies at different sites across the country. Where did our colleagues stand in comparison to others in our field?

Unfortunately, the results we found when surveying our own colleagues are mirrored in many schools. Students are disengaged from the research process and fail to see its relevance in their lives. Conner (2010) cites a variety of research articles explaining how our students entering college are, in great number, requiring remedial courses and "don't have the knowledge to conduct research or write an in-depth analysis paper" (p. 585). By building skills over several years, we're hoping to improve this issue with the students in our own schools, both those heading to college and those going into the workforce. In fact, in a 2004 report, the National Commission on Writing for America's Families, Schools, and Colleges shared its findings regarding businesses and salaried employees. Among the businesses, 51% said "they frequently or almost always take writing into consideration when hiring salaried employees" (2004, p. 9). Once hired, they will utilize their writing skills on the job, since 70% said that two-thirds of the salaried employees are responsible for writing (p. 7). When surveyed about the type of writing, companies claimed that technical writing is used by 59% of employees, and formal reports are used by 62% (p. 11).

Broskoske, who researched innovations to teaching research on the college level, commented on what we've been doing "wrong":

> Because many students lack a true grasp of the overall task, they also lack an understanding of how to proceed in preparing the paper. Without a sense of direction, students do not understand what to look for in the professional literature or how to present the information when they write.
>
> (2007, p. 31)

As a result, students sometimes are offtrack from the very beginning. Having a clearer understanding of what happens during effective research could aid students in knowing what, exactly, they're choosing a topic for. At present, students may be choosing topics to study for several weeks without a clear understanding of what they're going to need to do with those topics.

Several theories support the idea of building research in a series of steps, our overall goal in this project. Notable researchers include Eisenberg and Berkowitz, who presented the Big 6 (2012); Kuhlthau (2013), who offers her Model of Inquiry; and Stripling (2009), who identified research stages, particularly as they relate to primary sources. Figure 5.2 delineates the major tenets of each of those ideas.

Additionally, curricular alignment becomes increasingly important as more states adopt the Common Core Standards and prepare for their emphasis on research writing, which, in some states, will carry more weight than earlier versions of standards. In its call to tackle these standards, the International Reading Association emphasizes that teachers need to "Provide opportunities for students to write in response to reading across the curriculum. Provide research opportunities that involve reading both print and digital texts, and that require writing in response to reading" (p. 3). A research experience clearly addresses these growing needs for information literacy and evaluation of sources, and, ultimately, will be happening in varied content areas.

Current professional research emphasizes the need for collaborative professionalism. Richard DuFour is a leader in the study of teachers working together to make changes in their schools through professional learning communities (PLCs). "In a PLC, *collaboration* represents a systematic process in which teachers work together interdependently in order to *impact* their classroom

	Big 6	**Kuhlthau's Model of Inquiry**	**Stripling**
Overview	Employs higher-level thinking skills when using technology in a step-by-step manner to gather information ("Big 6 Skills Overview," 2012).	Emphasizes the student's tasks, thoughts, feelings, actions, and strategies during the research process.	What students learn through research has value and meaning. (Stripling).
Stages/ Phases	- Figuring out what research is needed - Determining quality sources - Finding the sources - Taking out the pertinent information - Organizing and sharing the information - Evaluating the steps and project/paper ("Big6 Skills Overview," 2012)	- Students realize what they do not know and get nervous about it. - Students have a topic and are ready to research. - Students are confused about the information that they find. - When students focus on their topics and information, they gain confidence. - As students find appropriate evidence, they gain interest. - Students clearly understand the topic and information, and they share their learning with others. (Kuhlthau)	- Questioning - Gathering information - Connecting with prior and new knowledge - Creating relationships with new information - Evaluating learning - Making connections to themselves and their learning (Stripling)

Figure 5.2 Frameworks for phases of inquiry

practice in ways that will lead to better results for their students, for their team, and for their school" (DuFour, DuFour, Eaker, & Many, 2006, p. 3). This is the kind of collaborative professionalism that we aim to employ through sharing our work with our own colleagues.

One key way to encourage lifelong learning with research is to root it in inquiry. "Inquiry-based learning is a form of project-based learning that capitalizes on the student's curiosity and proceeds with guided exploration of a topic. Students derive 'essential questions' for research, and the instructor(s) model the research process" (Buerkett, 2011, p. 21). Buerkett, a librarian, cites authors Kuhlthau, Maniotes, and Caspari, "Inquiry-based projects involve social collaboration and project discussion in multiple forums, so students develop lasting connections for lifelong learning" (p. 21). She has taken inquiry-based research a step further by using modern online tools as pieces in the process. She extols the virtues of online tools like Noodletools, which assists students in creating citations and developing notes, notecards, and outlines; Wallwisher, which allows students to collaborate on their research by posting questions online and receiving feedback; and Poll Everywhere, which allows teachers to gather information from students quickly using their cell phones.

Dobler (2012) agrees about the need for inquiry. In her work, she indicates, "To encourage inquiry, cultivate a sense of wonder within the classroom. Have students take on the role of a scientist, an expert, or a journalist, using their curiosity to guide their Internet investigation" (p. 20). Again, one way to ease our research burden is *inspiring* kids to research rather than just *requiring*.

Our Survey Results and the Helpful Matrix

Based on our research findings, from both the literature review and the first-hand collection of local data, we created a matrix for 7th through 12th grades, which lists each grade level and research skills that consensus showed were important at those grade levels. We then aligned it to the Common Core Writing Standards, making adjustments where necessary from what we created from survey results alone. Of course, when looking at the Common Core Standards, we were a bit shocked as to what younger students were expected to know, as this was not what our students typically had knowledge of when we taught research in our own classrooms. At the end of this matrix, we added a table that included some grade-level teaching strategies and some unique, inquiry-based project ideas that we shared with our ELA teachers, designed to help them get students engaged in research through questions and topics applicable to their own lives.

Building Research Skills by Using the Common Core Writing Standards

The Helpful Matrix of Research Skills and the Common Core Writing Standards (Figure 5.3) focuses on research skills that should be taught at each grade level to build on prior skills and knowledge throughout junior and

Grade Level	Research Skills	Common Core Standards
7	– Thesis statements (general) – Avoid plagiarism, including basic citation of sources – Find and summarize/quote/paraphrase sources (print and digital) – Use search terms effectively – Basics of search engines (e.g., they are not sources, they lead you to sources) – Assess credibility and accuracy of sources, including bias	W.7.1—Write arguments to support claims with clear reasons and relevant evidence W.7.2—Write informative/explanatory texts to examine a topic and convey ideas, concepts, and information through the selection, organization, and analysis of relevant content W.7.3—Write narratives to develop real or imagined experiences or events using effective technique, relevant descriptive details, and well-structured event sequences W.7.6—Use technology, including the Internet, to produce and publish writing **and link to and cite sources**, as well as to interact and collaborate with others, **including linking to and citing sources** W.7.7—Conduct short research projects to answer a question, drawing on several sources, and **generating additional related, focused questions for further research and investigation** W.7.8—Gather relevant information from multiple print and digital sources, using search terms effectively, assess the credibility **and accuracy** of each source, and quote or paraphrase the data and conclusions of others, while avoiding plagiarism and **following a standard format for citation** W.7.9—Draw evidence from literary or informational texts to support analysis, reflection, and research
8	– Build on seventh-grade skills – Evaluating sources – Taking notes from sources – Basics of source citation – Works cited (formal citation)	W.8.1—Write arguments to support claims with clear reasons and relevant evidence W.8.2—Write informative/explanatory texts to examine a topic and convey ideas, concepts, and information through the selection, organization, and analysis of relevant content W.8.3—Write narratives to develop real or imagined experiences or events using effective techniques, relevant descriptive details, and well-structured event sequences W.8.6- Use technology, including the Internet, to produce and publish writing and **present the relationships between information and ideas efficiently,** as well as to interact and collaborate with others W.8.7—Conduct short research projects to answer a question **(including a self-generated question)**, drawing on several sources and generating additional related, focused questions **that allow for multiple avenues of exploration** W.8.8—Gather relevant information from multiple print and digital sources, using search terms effectively, assess the credibility and accuracy of each source, and quote or paraphrase the data and conclusions of others, while avoiding plagiarism and following a standard format for citation W.8.9—Draw evidence from literary or informational texts to support analysis, reflection, and research

Figure 5.3 A helpful matrix of research skills and the Common Core Writing Standards

Grade Level	Research Skills	Common Core Standards
9	+Build on seventh- and eighth- grade skills - Narrow/broaden topics - Choosing the BEST sources from those students find - Synthesize multiple sources, including databases - Strengthen thesis statements - Strengthen note-taking for purpose/audience/task - Integrating sources into text	"W.9–10.1—Write arguments to support claims **in an analysis of substantive topics or texts, using valid reasoning** and relevant **and sufficient** evidence W.9–10.2—Write informative, explanatory texts to examine and convey **complex** ideas, concepts, and information **clearly and accurately** through the **effective** selection, organization, and analysis of content W.9–10.3—Write narratives to develop real or imagined experiences or events, using effective techniques, **well-chosen** details, and well-structured event sequences W.9–10.6—Use technology, including the Internet, to produce, publish, **and update individual or shared writing products, taking advantage of technology's capacity to link to other information, and to display information flexibly and dynamically** W.9–10.7—Conduct short, **as well as more sustained** research projects to answer a question (including a self-generated question) **or solve a problem; narrow or broaden the inquiry when appropriate; synthesize multiple sources on the subject, demonstrating understanding of the subject under investigation** W.9–10.8—Gather relevant information from multiple **authoritative** print and digital sources, using **advanced searches** effectively; assess the **usefulness** of each source **in answering the research question; integrate information into the text selectively to maintain the flow of ideas,** avoiding plagiarism and following a standard format for citation W.9–10.9—Draw evidence from literary or informational text to support analysis, reflection, and research"
10	+All skills from ninth grade repeated plus - In-text citations - MLA paper format (spacing, font size, headers, margins, etc.)	SEE W.9–10.1–3, 6–9

Figure 5.3 (*Continued*)

Grade Level	Research Skills	Common Core Standards
11	+Projects that include all previously taught elements of research - Formal paper and presentation - Specialized thesis statements - Evaluate sources for their applicability to purpose/audience/task - Strengthen note-taking for purpose/audience/task - Avoid overreliance on one source - Develop a topic of "current" interest (i.e., continuing flow of source material available)	"W.11–12.1—Write arguments to support claims in an analysis of substantive topics or texts, using valid reasoning and relevant and sufficient evidence W.11–12.2—Write informative, explanatory texts to examine and convey complex ideas, concepts, and information clearly and accurately through the effective selection, organization, and analysis of content W.11–12.3—Write narratives to develop real or imagined experiences or events, using effective technique, well-chosen details, and well-structured event sequences W.11–12.6—Use technology, including the Internet, to produce, publish, and update individual or shared writing products **in response to ongoing feedback, including new arguments or information** W.11–12.7—Conduct short, as well as more sustained research projects to answer a question (including a self-generated question) or solve a problem; narrow or broaden the inquiry when appropriate; synthesize multiple sources on the subject, demonstrating understanding of the subject under investigation W.11–12.8—Gather relevant information from multiple authoritative print and digital sources, using advanced searches effectively; assess **the strengths and limitations of each source, in terms of the task, purpose, and audience**; integrate information into the text selectively to maintain the flow of ideas, avoiding plagiarism and **overreliance on any one source** and following a standard format for citation W.11–12.9—Draw evidence from literary or informational text to support analysis, reflection, and research"
12	+Projects that include all previously taught elements of research - APA formatting	SEE W.11–12.1–3, 6–9 (same as previous level)

Figure 5.3 (*Continued*)

senior high school, the Common Core Writing Standards for 7th through 12th grades, and teaching strategies and project ideas for each grade level.

This list starts with what seventh graders are expected to do with the research part of writing, and these standards advance through the grade levels. All of these are focused on having students use multiple sources that have quality and credibility and citing them in a particular format when doing basic and advanced research projects. The matrix is broken down into grade levels, research skills, and the Common Core Standards. When identifying research skills, we broke down each standard into parts to make it more teacher-friendly. From grade level to grade level, these skills build on one another by using prior knowledge and applying these to new skills. You will notice that some words are bolded in the Common Core Standards section; these note the changes that were made to each level to make it more advanced. Figure 5.3 shows the finished matrix.

Adding to the Conversation

After the matrix was created, we shared it with ELA colleagues through emails, and solicited their feedback. We also offered authentic, engaging, inquiry-based ideas and products for research tasks to our ELA teachers at these grade levels, including some based on what is in our curricula beyond the English classroom.

Since our schools are structured a bit differently, we utilized different means of implementing the next steps. At Stacey's school, the principal asked the English department to come up with some ELA topics about writing, around which Stacey then created a series of 10-minute mini lessons by using handouts. Topics included MLA and APA formats, using a student-friendly writing rubric and how to adapt it, writing across the curriculum, and the five-paragraph essay with sample transitions. These lessons obviously made an impact on many of the faculty members, as they made additional copies of the session handouts and distributed them to their students.

In Karin's school, she followed up the matrix distribution by connecting with the language arts teachers in her building on an individual basis, asking their feedback about how the research matrix could help in their classrooms, how the matrix makes them think differently about how they may teach research, what was surprising and interesting about when and how research could be taught, and how the ideas for implementation might spur ideas different from what they had done before. One teacher said, "I love having this continuum! It helps me in my classroom by telling me exactly what I am responsible for teaching . . . [it] also lets me know what I don't have to cover with students because it will be covered in later classes." Another said that the matrix provides support for the "You're going to need this someday" argument that English teachers often use: "I can say to my 10th graders that by working on in-text citations, they will be well-prepared for the formal research paper they will be writing in their junior year."

Teachers also agreed that the matrix made them think differently about how they teach research skills. One said, "It helps me narrow my focus with students and gives me the structure to build research skills with my students." Another said, "The information in the continuum helped me feel less overwhelmed. Sometimes I feel like there is just so much to do in the junior year with the research paper, and breaking the process down into very manageable chunks/projects every year just makes sense." Additionally, many valued new ideas for teaching research skills we shared. A teacher commented, "Next year, I'd really like to try more of the suggested projects. I can see ninth graders really getting into 'A way to make my world better.'" Another teacher responded, "The ideas for implementation do spur activities that I have not done previously . . . Giving students a Works Cited page (eighth grade) and having them find the sources also allows them to see the purpose of how the Works Cited page is set up and its purpose in the first place."

When teaching these challenging skills, teachers can use any number of these strategies. We provided our ELA staff with strategies and project ideas aimed at spurring inquiry and engagement, rather than focusing on formal research writing. Some examples from the table include 24 Hours of Questions, in which students write down what questions they have about anything for a full day, or a Life Timeline of critical events in their lives to generate topics; scavenger hunts to find different types of sources; evaluating bogus websites; games about MLA format; and team competitions for taking quotes and making them into the best paraphrases or narrowing topics. Teachers can have students compare the research process to a legal case like Broskoske (2007) did in his classroom (pp. 31–32).

Also, some teachers are under the impression that writing an essay or term paper is the only way that research can be used, but there are many project ideas that can be applied, such as collages, musical playlists, creating games from the research that is found, making a public service announcement about a controversial issue, writing a narrative in which the setting has been researched (I-Journey, for example), or the I-Search (Macrorie, 1988).

Another example created by Bickens, Bittman, and Connor (2013) is the *Autobiography Project,* a multigenre narrative that includes many types of writing, from argument to research. It includes sections like Before I Was, There Was, in which students investigate what happened before they were born; My Origin and Culture, in which students research their backgrounds; and It's Not Fair, a persuasive piece requiring research and claims (pp. 43–49). These strategies and projects entice students to follow the inquiry process so that they are more likely to remember, apply, and value this information so they can utilize these skills in all grade levels and in college or the workforce. Because of this, teachers will be encouraged and renewed as well.

Research Is for Everyone!

In our own classrooms, we will continue to unfold and revise the way we teach research skills, but we also have a clear vision of what needs to happen in the near future to bring our project to the next level.

Our plan is to branch out to other content areas, as well as elementary schools, in our districts. We can begin this process by having conversations with interested teachers in other content areas, such as science and history, and by offering ideas for engaging research tasks that tie in to the topics they teach. There is a natural fit for cross-curricular research inherent in the matrix. Next, we would like to collaborate with elementary teachers to develop a matrix with teaching strategies and project ideas that would be applicable to their students, and to align our work and theirs.

Ultimately, the change we have started will come to fruition. As teachers implement these skills at each grade level, research will be less overwhelming for our kids. When we introduce a comprehensive, multi-page research task to our students in 11th or 12th grade, they will already be familiar with the pieces (Works Cited page, evaluating sources, etc.), and what we are doing will be familiar, giving us the opportunity to help them refine and deepen their research skills, not start from scratch. It will not be their first time evaluating a source or creating a Works Cited entry. We believe this plan will give students a strong foundation of skills that will assist them in the 21st century environment as employees, college students, and seekers of information. Also, it will aid teachers in understanding how critical these skills are, at an earlier grade level than they may realize, and how to teach them in a reasonable sequence.

References

Bickens, S., Bittman, F., & Connor, D. J. (2013). Developing academic skills through multigenre autobiography. *English Journal, 102*(5), 43–49.

Big 6 skills overview. (2012). *The Big 6: Information & Technology Skills for Student Success.* Retrieved from http://big6.com/pages/about/big6-skills-overview.php

Broskoske, S. L. (2007). Prove your case: A new approach to teaching research papers. *College Teaching, 55*(1), 31–32.

Buerkett, R. (2011). Inquiry and assessment using web 2.0 tools. *School Library Monthly, 28*(1), 21–24.

Conner, J. O. (2010, August). If you require it, will they learn from it? Student perceptions of an independent research project. *History Teacher, 43*(4), 585–594.

Dobler, E. (2012, August/September). Internet inquiry: Effective strategies to enhance critical inquiry skills. *Reading Today, 30*(1), 20–21.

DuFour, R., DuFour, R., Eaker, R., & Many, T. (2006). A guide to action for professional learning communities at work. In *Learning by Doing: A Handbook for Professional Learning Communities at Work* (pp. 1–12). Bloomington, IN: Solution Tree. Retrieved from http://pages.solution-tree.com/rs/solutiontree/images/lbd_freechapter.pdf

International Reading Association. (2012). *Literacy implementation guidance for the ELA Common Core State Standards.* Retrieved from www.reading.org/Libraries/association -documents/ira_ccss_guidelines.pdf

Kuhlthau, C. (2013). Information search process. Retrieved from http://comminfo.rutgers.edu/~kuhlthau/information_search_process.htm

Macrorie, K. (1988). *The I-Search paper.* Portsmouth, NH: Heineman.

National Commission on Writing for America's Families, Schools, and Colleges. (2004, September). *Writing: A ticket to work . . . or a ticket out. A survey of business leaders.* College Board.

Stripling, B. (2009). Teaching inquiry with primary sources. *TPS Quarterly.* The Library of Congress. Retrieved from www.loc.gov/teachers/tps/quarterly/inquiry_learning/article.html

CHAPTER

6 Connecting Teachers with Authentic Texts

Jane M. Spohn

Not a (Reading) Teacher

As a certified reading specialist and science teacher, I was constantly being reminded by some of the other content-area colleagues that they were NOT reading teachers. Often, these conversations included an assertion that some of my teaching activities were "fluffy" and lacked the rigor needed to support content learning. When I would counter by asking these teachers how much students engaged in reading and writing in their "more rigorous" classrooms, my colleagues would often break eye contact and mutter responses lamenting the lack of literacy skills their students brought to their classrooms.

One result of the shift to Common Core State Standards is that teachers across disciplines are finally realizing the need to be prepared to increase the rigor of literacy requirements and supports in their classrooms. However, many may not know exactly where to begin. Some teachers use round-robin reading, and others report they usually do most of the reading aloud, rather than asking students to tackle their texts. Some assign the reading to be done independently and then wonder why discussions are only led by a certain few students while the majority of the class opts not to respond at all. If these experiences paint a pained picture of reading in some content-area classrooms, just imagine what the writing assignments look like!

So began my mission to pull my colleagues into the cult of the literacy professional. I began with several guiding questions. What could happen if various texts were used alongside the official textbooks in all content classes? Could a team of teachers work together to make this idea a reality? What would be the results? This chapter delineates my efforts to address these issues and questions in my school building. I outlined a three-pronged plan to look at what the existing research said about cultivating a successful team approach, the nature of adolescent literacy, and the quality of types of texts that were most effective for instruction. My next step would be to compare these findings against the structures and beliefs in place in my own school building, and to bring the elements together into an initiative that would impact the quality of teaching and learning in our classrooms.

What They Need

Fang and Wei (2010) note that, "Students do not learn to read once and for all in the elementary school. They need to continue to develop their reading ability in order to deal with the more specialized and complex texts of secondary content areas" (p. 264). It is widely accepted that literacy development is a lifelong task. Considering this, we should expect, rather than lament, that students enter middle school and high school unprepared to read from, write about, think about, and discuss higher level texts. They need instruction and support to develop these skills and it is each teacher's role to supply that instruction within their own content teaching. Many educators know that students must read, write, think, and talk about what they are learning. Finding a balance between these areas and appropriate strategies to support each is the challenge, and one that can be effectively met by teacher collaboration.

However, simply providing opportunities for teachers to seek professional development is not adequate enough. Effective collaboration needs systematic support (National Center for Literacy Education, 2013). Educators must first embrace the concept of developing literacy within their content areas, with an overall goal of developing critical thinkers. For teachers who view themselves primarily as purveyors of specialized content, this signals a significant shift in thinking. Scholars argue that this type of change and (re)learning is the key to the success of school reform, and the most important outcome of teacher collaboration is improvement of teachers' instructional practice (Goddard, Goodard, & Tschannen-Moran, 2007).

Enter professional learning communities (PLCs). What are PLCs? PLCs involve sharing work-related ideas with a community of colleagues via digital or face-to-face communications for the betterment of one's professional practice (Perez, 2012). In a study by Shanahan and Shanahan (2008), PLCs were formed consisting of math, science, and history teachers, university professors, and literacy experts. These teams found that reading processes were specialized in specific content areas with focuses on varying skills (p. 49). Strengths of this varied team member approach were identifying the similarities and differences in literacy learning and then establishing learner supports. Collaboration is a key component in increasing student achievement, but focused collaboration is even more effective.

A study by Douglas Fisher, Nancy Frey, and Douglas Williams (2002) described how a PLC implemented "seven defensible strategies" over the course of three school years at a low achieving high school in California. Teachers across all content areas learned how to use the seven strategies in their specific content areas, and then began planning, teaching, and reflecting about their lessons and outcomes. The results were positive. The success of this structured approach of focusing on specific literacy strategies was due to the value the school placed on collaboration.

> The shared decisions of the staff development committee and school governance helped us articulate a school wide focus on instruction. Subsequent professional development has built the teachers' ability to implement each practice. The administration incorporates each strategy into accountability plans only after teachers have sufficient professional development on using the approach.
>
> (p. 73)

Our middle school team was already a PLC in action, if not yet by name. We were already meeting almost daily and discussing student growth, teaching strategies, and the nuts and bolts of daily life. I approached the principal with the idea of our team implementing mentor texts and supporting strategies across the content areas, of course citing some research to support the idea. He was receptive and wanted to be kept up to date on our plans to implement the ideas and then on future success. Our entire middle school team was now an official PLC.

Our team of four seventh grade and four eighth grade teachers and two learning support teachers met in our official PLC twice a week for 25 minutes each, as well as other times as needed. We share a morning common planning time from 8:00–8:45, as well as an afternoon time from 2:50–3:20. This planning time was already in place and being utilized before we began turning our focus toward the tasks of incorporating mentor texts. The structure allowed for biweekly PLC meetings for planning and sharing ideas and strategies for implementing our new texts. It also allowed us time to reflect as I kept notes while teachers shared about using their texts and strategies. It was time well spent, as teachers shared mostly success stories about student engagement and higher levels of thinking through writing and discussion.

Why did we expect to be successful? Because we had everything that the research tells us is needed for such a venture. We had time and opportunity to collaborate as a PLC, which is one of the major obstacles in many educational settings. We had financial support for resources needed to meet our goals of implementing the use of mentor and authentic texts, and the support of our administration. We had compiled numerous literacy strategies for vocabulary, comprehension, and writing to choose from as we began our work, and we aligned our work with the Common Core Standards as we focused on increasing the rigor of literacy use. In short, we were professionally poised to kick butt. Could this team make a difference in the lives of seventh and eighth grade learners? Was it possible to begin to seriously prepare them for college or the workforce in their middle school years? Now that we were assembled and equipped, we began to explore the core of most academic reading: the textbook.

Reading Fresh, Reading Healthy

Most educators would agree that their school's selected textbooks are solid sources of generalized and summarized content information, but are overall bland and dry. Barry compares the textbook to primary texts as "the difference between fresh and canned peas" (2010, p. 44). If we can serve up fresh, engaging reading, then teachers need to move away from the canned textbook as a crutch for every lesson. Not only do teachers have primary sources as valuable teaching resources, they have numerous texts that can be used in connection with textbook learning. Authentic texts are available for any content at any level with the right amount of searching. It is worth your time to find these resources that will build students' reading, writing, speaking, and listening skills, as long as you provide appropriate scaffolding for the reading. It is not enough to say, "You will need this for college" or simply, "You will need this someday." Making an effort to connect classroom learning to the real world goes a long way to making reading more palatable, in an old-world style.

Even though our team of teachers had worked closely over the course of several years with the same teachers spanning that time, I didn't know exactly all the ins and outs of everyone's lesson planning and teaching styles. I decided to create a survey that would gather data about the types of texts students worked with, as well as the formats and quality of writing used in each classroom. Another goal of the survey was to generate some thought in my fellow teachers about possibilities they might not have considered using in their lessons. Instead of sitting them down and talking at them, telling them what I thought would be valuable to our students, I wanted them to come to the table with some ideas of their own. As they took the survey during our first in-service day, I heard some comments that mainly centered on the time it would take to work outside of the textbook, or to use writing on a daily basis. But then, just as I hoped, I heard other comments about the possibility of students becoming more engaged if they provided texts outside of the textbook. We were headed in the right direction.

According to the results of the initial survey (see Table 6.1), we noticed that our teachers utilized textbooks for the majority of reading material, with some primary and secondary sources layered in. There was a definite lack of the use of mentor texts (defined by Dorfman and Cappelli, 2007). Mentor texts provide strong examples of writing from the real world that teachers can use

Table 6.1 Text use: Survey results

5 is always, 4 is often, 3 is sometimes, 2 is seldom, and 1 is never	Initial Survey Average Scores	Post Survey Average Scores
Teacher Behavior: Text Use		
I use the textbook as the main text to teach my course.	4.25	3.4
I use digital sources of information to support my lessons.	3.57	4.25
I use works of fiction to support my lessons.	2.2	3.5
I use nonfiction texts to support my lessons.	2.3	4.0
I use primary and secondary documents to support my lessons.	2.5	3.25
I use visual documents to support my lessons.	2.4	2.75
Teacher Behavior: Writing		
The strategies I use in my lessons require students to write daily.	4.28	4.5
I feel that I use many forms of writing in my lessons.	3.7	4.5
I feel I have had enough training on how to use writing in my courses.	3.57	4.1
Students summarize what they learned through writing in my lessons.	3.85	4.5
Students' writing demonstrates higher level thinking.	3	4.33
I feel that students know how to write well.	2.28	3.5
I feel that using writing in my lessons is time well spent.	4.1	4.66

to bridge the gap between classroom learning and everyday experience. After looking at the results, our team agreed that we could be offering our students more in the way of reading materials with greater variety and breadth. The team created a "wish list" of mentor texts to use in their content lessons, the majority being nonfiction. Our state test results consistently showed lower scores on average in students' ability to analyze nonfiction, so it just made sense to help them develop that skill outside of reading class. Also, some of the teachers already incorporated several historical fiction titles, so we decided to target nonfiction.

We explored a range of booklists that were available on websites such as Good Reads (www.goodreads.com) and the Young Adult Library Service Association (YALSA) (www.ala.org/yalsa/booklistsawards/booklistsbook). We skimmed content-area reading textbooks with a new purpose: searching for annotated bibliographies and suggested books. Specifically, we were looking for texts that we felt would provide a real world connection to our content while demonstrating the types of writing done by professionals across content areas. Over a few weeks, we were able to research and find titles that fit our ideals for each content area, as well as ensuring they meshed with our state and Common Core standards. We turned first to our area libraries to locate some of the books on our lists. Other titles had online samples of pages through Amazon (www.amazon.com), and a few of the titles were abandoned after taking a closer look at the volumes themselves or the sample pages, due to text complexity (too easy or difficult). We wrote a proposal to the Endless Mountains Writing Project, a National Writing Project affiliate, which was accepted, and we were then able to purchase the remaining titles, so our plan was one step closer to implementation. Table 6.2 delineates our final book list for this project.

Table 6.2 Selected mentor texts by content area

Math	Science	Social Studies
Secrets of Mental Math: The Mathemagician's Secrets to Lightning Calculations and Mental Math Tricks by Arthur Benjamin and Michael Shermer	*Animal Defenses: How Animals Protect Themselves* by Etta Kaner and Pat Stephens	*A Kid's Guide to America's Bill of Rights: Curfews, Censorship and the 100 Pound Giant* by Kathleen Krull

(Continued)

Table 6.2 Continued

Math	Science	Social Studies
Math Doesn't Suck: How to Survive Middle School Math Without Losing Your Mind or Breaking a Nail by Danica McKellar	*A Drop of Water* by Walter Wick	*Teens on Trial: Young People Who Challenged the Law— And Changed Your Life* by Thomas A. Jacobs
The Great Number Rumble: A Story of Math in Surprising Places by Cora Lee, Gillian O'Reilly, and Virginia Gray	*Science Verse* by Jon Scieszka and Lane Smith	*History Puzzle: An Interactive Visual Timeline* by Cherry Denman
One Grain of Rice: A Mathematical Folktale by Demi	*Science Warriors: The Battle Against Invasive Species* by Sneed B. Collard III	*P is for Passport: A World's Alphabet* by Devin Scillian
Mathcurse by Jon Scieszka and Lane Smith	*Phenomena: Secrets of the Senses* by Donna M. Jackson	*The Folks in the Valley: A PA Dutch ABC* by Jim Aylesworth and Stefano Vitale
	G is for Galaxy: An Out of This World Alphabet by Janis Campbell, Cathy Collison, and Alan Stacy	*The Cartoon History of the United States* by Larry Gonick
	V is for Vanishing: An Alphabet of Endangered Animals by Patricia Mullins	*Cleopatra VII: Daughter of the Nile* by Christiana Gregory
	Q is for Quark: A Science Alphabet Book by David M. Schwartz	
	Animalia by Graeme Base	
	The Cartoon Guide for Chemistry and *The Cartoon Guide to the Environment* by Larry Gonick	
	Silent Spring by Rachel Carson	
	Inherit the Wind by Jerome Lawrence and Robert E. Lee	
	Growing up in Coal Country by Susan Campbell Bartoletti	

Scaffolding through Strategy Use

In order to use the books effectively, the next step was to identify reading and writing strategies to support students in content learning. Our lesson planning already included essential questions, and activating, teaching, summarizing, and extending thinking strategies. How could we possibly have any areas of weakness with all of that in place? Our focus needed to be on incorporating strategies that truly supported student learning, instead of filling a lesson planning requirement. We decided that strategies may look good on paper, but we needed to be certain that deep thinking would be a product of their use and not simply surface level learning. This realization made us take a long, hard look at what we do on a daily basis in our classrooms. It also made us realize in order to meet the requirements of the Common Core, we had to "kick it up a notch" when it came to literacy. Strategies we decided that would provide the scaffolding needed to meet the rigor of the Common Core and would help develop deeper learning are listed in Table 6.3.

Professional Learning Community . . . That's Us!

We had new supplemental texts, a compiled repertoire of strategies for full-fledged literacy infusions, and a team of teachers primed and pumped for bringing them together with the curriculum. In this next section, you will find out how our plan unfolded across classrooms.

Table 6.3 Literacy strategies that use higher-order thinking

Vocabulary	Comprehension	Writing to Learn
Interactive Word Walls	Previewing	Double-Entry Notes
Frayer Squares	Prediction Charts	Summarizing
Word Sorts	KWL	T-Charts
Vocabulary Notebooks/ Journals	SQ3R	Foldables
Cornell Notes	Partner, Shared, and Close Reading	Letter to Teacher or Absent Student
Semantic Feature Analysis	Journaling	Quick Writes
Knowledge Rating Scales	Compare/Contrast Charts	Chapter Summary Templates
Morphemic Analysis	Cause and Effect Charts	RAFT Writing
Word Origin Analysis	Timelines	Acrostic Poems

In eighth grade ecology class, our curriculum focused on natural resources and fossil fuels. The textbook provided highlighted vocabulary, graphs, charts, and tables, enticing pictures and photographs, and questions that accompanied each section. For this unit, the eighth grade science teacher chose to read *Growing up in Coal Country* by Susan Campbell Bartoletti, which had originally been selected for social studies and could also be used in that area. Bartoletti's text uses personal memoirs, as she collected oral histories of many turn-of-the-century coal workers and their families. Included are stories from the "breaker boys," who were young children, usually ages 8–12, sent into the mines to break coal into uniform-sized chunks. The stories, accompanied by black and white photos, made personal connections with the students. Pennsylvania was a top coal producer, and, 100 years ago, any one of the boys in the class could have been a breaker boy, working 12- to 14-hour shifts, 6 days a week.

As students kept double-entry notes where they would summarize on the left and make personal connections or ask questions on the right, many questions were raised and family histories were shared. This connection spilled over into their history class, as many students wanted to know more about child labor laws, unions, and the rapid immigration to the United States for employment in the coal industry. The section on coal mining in the textbook is only several pages long. They would have learned about fossil fuels and how they were formed over millions of years, but the connections to the Bartoletti text were much deeper and promoted higher level thinking and writing.

Reading this text led to a field trip, during which students measured the acidity of local rivers, streams, and creeks, due to acid mine drainage. Students visited four sites and collected data (such as the pH levels), soil and rock samples, and insects and small organisms, and took notes about each site and their findings. In other words, they thought like scientists, did work as scientists, and wrote like scientists. The Common Core demands that the students' skill set contains skills that will take them into the real world. Teachers commented that they had never seen students so engaged on a field trip. They were each collecting their samples and writing in journals—in other words, staying on task and completing their assigned roles and LEARNING. The next day was spent analyzing the data and forming conclusions about the state of the local water. This is an experience these students will remember as adults. Deep learning and higher-order thinking trumps textbook-driven lessons any day.

In the social studies curriculum, the Constitution and Bill of Rights was examined in depth. Students had access to the language of the real documents and the teacher guided them through, making connections to our lives today. After understanding the composition of our government and how the judicial system works, *Teens on Trial* by Thomas A. Jacobs was used for students to connect to how the law can affect their lives and the lives of their friends. The Bill of Rights was explored at a deeper level with connections to America's teens through *A Kid's Guide to America's Bill of Rights: Curfews, Censorship and the 100 Pound Giant* by Kathleen Krull. In math, seventh graders exploring exponents read *One Grain of Rice* by Demi, and saw how a young girl used her number sense to outsmart the raja, saving her village and people. Seventh graders were also exposed to a plethora of sources about the Holocaust as they completed a cross-curricular research unit involving their history, language arts, and reading classes. Biographies, autobiographies, memoirs, diaries, historical fiction, newspaper articles, personal letters, government propaganda posters, plays, poetry, and numerous websites were used over the course of a marking period. Students completed daily reading and writing about events and people during the Holocaust, using higher-order thinking as they made connections across texts and genres. In the eighth grade, a slavery unit was the foundation of the research project, again using numerous titles and genres of text.

Next, we incorporated the plan in a seventh grade world cultures classroom. Ancient civilizations can be fascinating to many students, yet not for others. Again, a textbook with all the bells and whistles was purchased just 2 years ago. It paints a detailed picture of Egyptians and their culture and religion. Connections are made to their technological advancements. Pyramids are shown as a marvel of their time. Yet, some students still are not engaged and voice that the information is boring. "Who cares about the past? It's ancient history!" Giggles filled the room. Enter the historical fiction text, *Cleopatra VII, Daughter of the Nile* by Christiana Gregory. This is a diary of 12-year-old Cleopatra as she struggles with her father's assassination attempts and a power hungry older sister. Written in the voice of someone their own age, students were drawn to her life and culture as the tell-all diary swept them back into a time that the world cultures book covers, but doesn't uncover, as the diary does. Students used a chapter graphic organizer that included drawing a picture, using context to work with vocabulary, descriptions of characters, and a summary of the reading for the day, as shown in Figure 6.1. The chapter summaries demonstrated that students were thinking deeply about the culture and region. With only 2 years to compare, the world cultures teacher felt that this time around, students had a deeper understanding of ancient Egyptian life and the impact it had on today's society.

Alphabet books were selected as mentor texts in science and history (see Table 6.2). Students were exposed to the simple format of each letter of the alphabet pertaining to a specific topic of interest. Astronomy was explored in *G is for Galaxy*. Chemistry was taken to a new level in *Q is for Quarks. V is for Vanishing* told of endangered species and the responsibilities humans have to keep them safe. World travel was made possible in *P is for Passport*. Our

Connecting Teachers with Authentic Texts

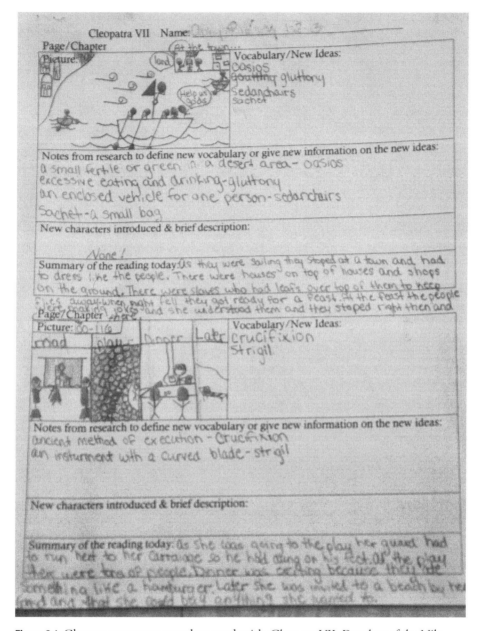

Figure 6.1 Chapter summary template used with *Cleopatra VII, Daughter of the Nile*

Pennsylvania Dutch region was explored in *The Folks in the Valley: A Pennsylvania Dutch Alphabet*. Multiple exposures to the alphabet book format gave the seventh and eighth grade language arts teachers an idea. Their year-end final project was to create an alphabet book describing learning that occurred from any and all student learning maps, unit essential questions, and lesson essential

Jane M. Spohn

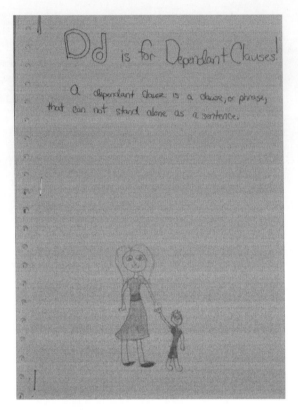

Figure 6.2 Student-generated alphabet book project samples

questions. Students brainstormed ideas for a day, created rough draft pages using a template, and then crafted final copies using old dot-matrix computer paper for the pages. The ream of paper consisting of endless connected pages provided the perfect amount of space for an ABC book, and a perfect way to use the reams we had stored for years. An example is provided in Figure 6.2. Examine the rubric and then the examples. Do you see evidence of student learning?

In Your School

Hopefully, this chapter has provided the spark needed to ignite your interest in providing authentic texts in your lessons. Selecting the texts and using sound scaffolding through strategy use is not a small task. This is not a road you should travel alone. Maybe you don't have common planning time already designated like my school does. This needs to be your first focus. I implore administrators to see the value in scheduling time for teachers to collaborate. Not just disciplinary teams, but cross-curricular teams that can provide varying perspectives on students, reading, writing and thinking strategies, and text use. This has to come from the top. Teachers are far too busy to place value on changing schedules just to find time to meet with one another. This needs to be done for you so you can concentrate on how to make this collaboration meaningful.

Talking with other teachers across the disciplines is necessary for teacher and student growth. You need to take the time and dig deeply into the Common Core to ensure the tasks you assign meet the high expectations that are set for students. The chances are good that many of the Common Core goals already align a good deal with what you already value, but if you are new to the literacy end of teaching, then they should serve as a structured guide. Create a literacy-rich classroom with access to many forms of written materials, but provide the scaffolding necessary for students to tackle the texts. Work with words and their meanings in context instead of in isolation, and write every day. If I were a doctor, this would be my prescription for you to create active, healthy readers, writers, and thinkers. Students deserve to get the most out of their time at school. More importantly, teachers deserve to feel pride in what they do because we all know some days it can be a thankless career. I wish you the best in your adventures and hope that someday, you, too, will share success stories of how you got students to think deeper through the use of authentic texts.

References

Barry, C. (2010). From great texts—to great thinking. *Educational Leadership, 67*(6), 42–46.

Dorfman, L., & Cappelli R. (2007). *Mentor texts: Teaching writing through children's literature.* Portland, ME: Stenhouse Publishers.

Fang, Z., & Wei, Y. (2010). Improving middle school students' science literacy through reading infusion. *The Journal of Educational Research, 103*, 262–273.

Fisher, D., Frey, N., & Williams, D. (2002, November). Reading and writing in the content areas: Seven literacy strategies that work. *Educational Leadership, 60*(3), 70–73.

Goddard, Y. L., Goodard, R. D., & Tschannen-Moran, M. (2007, April). A theoretical and empirical investigation of teacher collaboration for school improvement and student achievement in public schools. *Teachers College Record, 109*(4), 877–896.

National Center for Literacy Education. (2013). Remodeling literacy learning: Making room for what works. Retrieved from www.nwp.org/cs/public/print/resource/4098

Perez, L. (2012, January–February). Innovative professional development: Expanding your professional learning network. *Knowledge Quest, 40*(3), 20–22.

Shanahan, T., & Shanahan, C. (2008). Teaching disciplinary literacy to adolescents: Rethinking content-area literacy. *Harvard Educational Review, 78*(1), 40–59.

CHAPTER

Connecting Content
The True Story of Dead End
Cindy Lisowski

Dead End or U-Turn?

The early years of my teaching career were characterized by isolation from my coworkers. This wasn't a conscious choice on my part or theirs, really—it was just how the school was structured then. It began with my first teaching assignment, and I was hit with the realization that I didn't have much background in the way of historical knowledge for many of the literary classics I was going to teach. For example, *The Great Gatsby* is often read at the junior level in high schools. My knowledge of the American 1920s was not significantly greater than that of my students. This was in those dusty days of the pre-Google world, when access to such resources was not exactly limited but was certainly not as easily accessible as it is today.

I found myself knocking on the door of a colleague, a history teacher who had the level of expertise for which I was looking. It was a move that would have incredible impact on my teaching. From that moment on, I was part of a dynamic cross-curricular duo. We talked, created, planned, improvised, persevered, and we succeeded in increasing our students' learning. Not only did we team-teach, we inspired and taught one another. No longer a lone English teacher with an inadequate history background, I now had an incredible, nonjudgmental resource who never shamed me about any lack of knowledge, a partner willing to work with me and happy to share from her deep content reserves. A rich, lifelong friendship developed and continues to thrive.

Fast forward 10 years with some minor changes: my friend is happily retired (actually volunteering at school, doing what she loves), and I am now a school librarian. One thing hasn't changed: we still enjoy reading and discussing books together. Last summer, we read *Dead End in Norvelt,* Jack Gantos's Newbery Medal–winning novel. We immediately saw so many ways that this book could blossom into an excellent cross-curricular project. With a new year on the horizon and such exciting possibilities in the air, I approached my school administrator about organizing a multidisciplinary team to tackle the novel. While my principal acknowledged that the project had some strong teaching potential, he was a bit hesitant at first, since in our school, as in every other public school in the United States, scores on the state assessment tests were high on the priority list. It seemed at first that my idea (which I would come to think of as "the Gantos project") would join some others on the back burner.

Instead of accepting the need to prepare for state testing as an obstacle and giving up hope of moving forward with my idea, I used the needs identified by the state test (at the time, it was the Pennsylvania State Assessment, or PSSA) as a rationale for moving forward with it. At my small, rural school (approximate student population, 485) for the preceding 2 years, eighth grade students had scored below 60% proficient on the state writing assessment. Writing was clearly an instructional need for our students. My principal was a bit more receptive after I shared this reasoning, but I soon hit another wall: the eighth grade teachers that I approached felt that they had too much to cover in their curriculum already and were not willing to take on my project.

And then, we (my retired friend and I) hit on a marvelous idea. The post-PSSA testing window at our school comes at the end of the year and is traditionally a time our staff has identified as being more fragmented than any other during the year. *WHAT IF* I worked with a team of teachers to read the novel and plan a cross-curricular unit over the course of the school year but we targeted that time period to actually implement the unit? Better yet, since the scores from the eighth grade testing indicated that writing was an area of need, *WHAT IF* the teacher team was composed of seventh grade teachers? The project would bring cohesion to end-of-year instruction and would also be preparing students just prior to their eighth grade year. Drawing on every bit of the perseverance I had developed and honed over all those years of team-teaching, I contacted the seventh grade teachers, posed the idea, and held my breath. The response was both immediate and positive: they were up to the challenge!

Road Work, Next Five Miles

In this chapter, I will outline my efforts to design and implement themed cross-curricular instruction in my school, with the unifying thread being *Dead End in Norvelt*. The goal of this project was to take a piece of quality literature and have a teacher team present it immediately after the state tests, when both teachers and students often just want the school year to be over—the educational wastelands. *Dead End in Norvelt* (which won the Newbery Medal in 2012) was selected in particular because Gantos, a native Pennsylvania writer, uses a small Pennsylvania town for the setting. The text mirrors many of the experiences of our seventh grade students who, like the novel's main character, are growing up in rural Pennsylvania.

The demographic group for this project included 56 seventh grade students and both the seventh grade English and history teachers. In addition, two special education teachers—one a gifted teacher and the other an emotional support teacher—plus me, the school librarian, rounded out the teacher team. Team teachers focused on content related themes emanating from the novel, and shared the planning for instruction and assessments. The Gantos project was designed from the ground up to be a joint venture in which teachers worked in their content areas but also together, as collaborators.

The project took place over the 2012–2013 school year. Students read the novel independently and participated in literature circles with their English teacher. The history teacher provided relevant historical background knowledge, such as lessons on the Great Depression, Franklin and Eleanor Roosevelt, and America in the 1960s. Other novel themes provided opportunities for outside experts and guest speakers to interact with the students. For example, in the Gantos novel, the narrator and his father go deer hunting, so we invited a local Pennsylvania Game Commission officer, Robert Minnich, to speak to the seventh grade class about the history of the game commission, local animals, and hunting.

Another novel theme was the Hells Angels motorcycle gang. They both visit and terrorize Norvelt, the novel's setting. The gang's signature motorcycle, Harley-Davidson, has a local franchise in our town. On an awesome June day, one of their mechanics thundered in via motorcycle to our school. He shared the company's history, unique design specs, and his Harley training experience. His presentation forced both teachers and students outside.

Stay in Lane: What the Research Says

There are a lot of strong reasons to explore teacher collaboration and cross-curricular teaching, particularly if we want to meet the needs of more students.

Teachers work with the entire gamut of student skill levels and abilities. Our students are not a homogeneous population. Differentiation is the educational answer: it allows teachers to meet student needs by tapping into student interests and learning styles. "Differentiated instruction stimulates creativity and helps students understand ideas at higher levels of thinking" (De Jesus, 2012). As teachers, we want creative, engaged students who can push into higher level, deep thinking. Cross-curricular projects provide a differentiated bonanza for teachers and students for both learning and assessment. If we allow students to play to their strengths, won't they perform with greater success? "Most of us as writers have our strengths and weaknesses. So do students. If you teach writing, you find people who are excellent spellers and understand the mechanics of grammar and don't say a thing. Others have voices. Some are very organized. Some are totally disorganized. I've taught first grade through graduate school. There's just an enormous range at every level" (Donald Murray, in *Because Writing Matters,* 2003, p. 13).

Student-centered learning is one of the most significant changes in education. Having choice empowers learners. In *Reading & Writing & Teens: A Parent's Guide to Adolescent Literacy* (2010), Fleischer questions how to motivate teens and notes, "there is a big role for adults, both teachers and parents, in this approach: helping to create an environment of choice, helping students find options for reading and writing that appeal to their interests, nudging teens toward interesting alternatives they may not have considered, or just being supportive of any literacy activity that attracts them" (p. 6). Student choice is a key component most strongly identified with building 21st-century literacies, according to a National Council of Teachers of English report (*Writing Between the Lines*, 2009, p. 2). Student choice is also at the heart of cross-curricular projects. Students need and like to have options, just as adults do.

Another need for both students and teachers is collaboration. Library media specialist and writer Buzzeo recommends that teachers "Find a way to establish—or improve—your collaborative practice, guided by the data that reveals your students' academic challenges and documents the essential nature of your work to help them to overcome these challenges and achieve" (Buzzeo & Wilson, 2007, p. 23). To Buzzeo's words, my principal would sing, "yes!" A great deal of our professional time in school revolves around student data. It makes sense to come together to understand what our students know and still need to learn. The scholarly community values data, as well. The National Center for Literacy Education (NCLE) looks at the new Common Core State Standards and highlights "Shared responsibility for students' literacy development . . . At their very core, then, these new standards require that teachers across all grades, and especially across the various disciplines, collectively assume responsibility for elevating literacy learning" (*Remodeling Literacy Learning,* 2013, p. 10). Currently, teachers collaborate to look at and analyze student data. This collaboration will need to expand for teachers to work together to meet the new Common Core Standards across the curriculum. Cross-curricular projects can be used to meet this need.

According to the Nation's Report Card, "Fifty-four percent of eighth-graders performed at the Basic level in writing in 2011" (2011, p. 10). Clearly, the data shows this is a need with less than half the nation's population of eighth graders writing at the proficient level. Since the Common Core Standards require student writing across the content areas, this need was even more urgently felt. When I worked as an English teacher, I became aware of content teachers' reluctance to have students write. Many teachers were uncomfortable with evaluating student writing and were concerned about the time it could take away from their instruction. The content teachers on my Gantos team were different in that they were comfortable with having students write in their classrooms. However, they were still not comfortable teaching about or grading student writing, so I knew that I would have to provide some direction and support in those areas.

Merge Right

My goal for this project was to elicit teacher enthusiasm with creative, self-selected student projects centered on a piece of young adult literature. I needed the language arts and history teachers, but also wanted to bring in as many other content areas as possible. I asked teachers of science, math, art, music, and physical education. No surprise for public school teachers, scheduling was a huge problem. The art teacher was interested but not scheduled to work with the seventh grade; music and physical education were only partial-year classes. In the end, the history and language arts teachers were the most involved, along with the gifted teacher and a special education teacher. I surveyed the teacher team to get their perspectives on teacher collaboration. My goals were to ascertain both their perspective and experience with teacher collaboration. I wanted to know if they knew what topics and information was covered by other content teachers of the same grade. I wanted to know if they had previously collaborated with the school librarian. The survey results are included as Figure 7.1.

Two smaller offshoots of this project were completed by the family consumer science teacher and also one of our music teachers. One group of the seventh grade students made mock Girl Scout Cookies. Characters in the novel sell Girl Scout Cookies, and they play a crucial role in several murders. Another

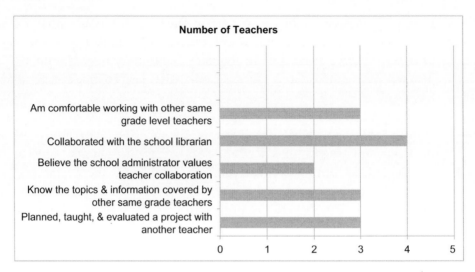

Figure 7.1 Baseline results of teacher survey

group created podcasts of the music from the 1960s, which was the time period of our novel. Unfortunately, the teacher involved with the podcasts was a shared music teacher who is only in our school on alternate days. So, even though one group of seventh graders learned about the music of the 1960s, the entire group did not. And because this teacher was not part of the team, he was unaware of the opportunity to present this to the rest of the teachers and students.

I actively worked with both the language arts and history teachers. In order to find time for collaboration, we had to be creative, persistent, and flexible. Our teacher team met for a working lunch to find common planning time. I learned that sometimes having 10 or 15 minutes for collaborating works, and sometimes just meeting with part of the team works as well. When I first began collaborating with my colleague (the history teacher), we met both before and after school. We were fortunate that we lived close to the school and that neither one of us had family demands forcing us home at specific times. Impromptu collaboration can occur in the school hallways, where teachers are posted outside the classroom doors.

The idea is this: collaborating becomes a priority, so you make it work. Even though teachers can be physically apart, today we have digital options enabling us to stay connected with texting and emailing, which are less intrusive and more immediate. I helped begin the novel unit. To spark student interest, the language arts teacher began the novel unit with historic and novel artifacts filling small shopping bags. Student groups unpacked, classified, and made predictions based on these items. In one bag, we had pictures of the Girl Scout logo, a white-tailed deer, former First Lady Eleanor Roosevelt, a website for arthritis, and a replica of the Newbery Medal. Our teacher team collaborated and designed a differentiated project grid that provided students with diverse options (see Figure 7.2).

Writing	Research	Project
Write a critical book review of the novel. Included must be your personal rating of the book with reasons why, and your recommendations as to who should read the novel.	Read a biography of Eleanor Roosevelt and find 2 more sources about her. Create a top-10 list of her greatest accomplishments as First Lady. Provide a reference for each accomplishment and a brief summary.	Video-taped author interview 2 Person presentation Mandatory dress rehearsal with script and teacher-approved content.
Diary entries. You are the narrator. Write about your life with your feuding parents or about life in Norvelt.	Research Alphabet Soup agencies New Deal programs Housing/Norvelt: Write an outline explaining the community details of towns such as Norvelt.	Create map or diorama of Norvelt based on research
Write 5 different types of poems connected to the novel. These must be original and printed separately. You may add graphics or sound.	UFOs in Pennsylvania: Read a book and find other sources about UFOs reported during the 1960s. Write an outline of your research	Survey MHS students about their belief in UFOs. Present findings visually on a chart or graph.
Write a skit connected to the book. It will contain dialogue with at least 2 people involved. Skit duration should be 5–6 minutes long.	Research Depression recipes: - Create grocery list - Price analysis of ingredients - Must include 3 references	Create a board game based on the novel. Write the instructions as well. Create an evaluation rubric for your project.
	PA Game Commission: Research its origin and the Hunter Safety Program. Create a brochure explaining both using facts.	Set up a taste test of recipes from the 1930s. Provide the recipes and a list of the ingredients

Figure 7.2 Differentiated project grid for assignment options for *Dead End in Norvelt*

> **Daily Reading Log**
>
> Name:
>
> *Dead End in Norvelt*   Date:
>
> Today I started at page:
>
> I finished at page:

Figure 7.3 Template for daily reading logs

Students had to complete one project for the language arts teacher and another for the history teacher. We were on a tight schedule with limited classes and end-of-the-year activities, such as field trips and special assemblies, plus, our teachers were required to give students another round of computer-mediated diagnostic tests (CDTs) to chart their progress on PSSA-like tasks. I helped develop an independent reading schedule for the seventh grade students and a daily reading log (see Figure 7.3). Students were assigned to literature circles by their language arts teacher. About every third class on the schedule, the students met in literature circles to discuss their reading. They came armed with role sheets, which they filled out as they read independently. This gave the students more room with greater privacy, and also gave me an opportunity to help monitor the groups. With the history teacher, I helped design project rubrics, provided the library resources, and helped guide student inquiry. I also helped with final project assessments.

I instructed the history students on writing personal thank you letters as they wrote to two different guest presenters. We had the Pennsylvania Game Commission officer, and also a representative from our local Harley-Davidson business. I created a post-project student feedback form, which the classes filled out after sharing their final researched projects (see Figure 7.4).

Student feedback was mostly positive, with 75% of the students happy with their project choice. A slightly higher percentage, 79% were happy with their finished project. Some of the skills students said they lacked were typing, computer skills, and putting sound or music into PowerPoint presentations. Students struggled with writing follow-up questions for the author interviews. The majority of students (79%) said they liked having a project where their teachers worked together. In the words of a wise student, "Yes. They want us to get along and be able to count on each other. I think it's good for them to do the same."

> 1. I was (happy or unhappy) with my project choice because . . .
>
> 2. I (lacked or possessed) the necessary skills to complete this project.
>
> 3. If skills were lacking, please explain what these were.
>
> 4. I was (happy or unhappy) with my finished project because . . .
>
> 5. If given the chance to do this again, what would I have done differently? Explain why.
>
> 6. What other projects would you have added to this?
>
> 7. Did you like having a project where your teachers worked together? Why?

Figure 7.4 Student survey about the Gantos project

Pass with Care

Looking back at this experience, I think there are numerous ways that I could take this work to a more complex level. At the high school level, one way to add complexity would be to increase the number of participating teachers and expand the project to include math, science, art, music, physical education, and family consumer science. If school scheduling could be made more flexible, this could increase the breadth and width of the project connections. If greater administrative support were given, such as time allotted for common teacher planning time, perhaps greater teacher investment would follow. Several teachers were not willing to get involved. Another extension option would be to work digitally with students from other schools. This would provide students with greater collaboration opportunities and an authentic audience for their writing and projects. Student project options could become more complex with greater Common Core connections and more digital project options, such as web quests or the designing of video games.

Virtual field trips to Norvelt and locations connected to Eleanor Roosevelt or the novel could be included. Students could write personal letters to author Jack Gantos, asking specific writing questions based on the novel. Students could debate the merit of the novel for the Newbery Medal. With future use of this unit, students could also be assigned to read Gantos's follow up, *From Norvelt to Nowhere,* which was released after our school year.

As far as addressing the needs for particular student populations, our gifted team teacher felt the web quest or game design options would be popular with the gifted students; however, her end-of-the-year schedule did not make either possible for the first round of our project. An English language learner student and his ELL teacher were initially worried about being successful with the project. By the end, both were happy and eager to share that it provided the student with a wide range of experience with language skills, writing, and research opportunities as the young man created a brochure with publishing software. They were both delighted with the quality of the finished project, as well as the learning and skill building along the way. The emotional support teacher on our team tapped into her passion and knowledge of history to show her self-contained classroom several YouTube videos connected to the novel's time period. For example, she showed *The Red Scare, The Day of the Triffids,* and *Sink the Bismarck*.

Many students selected projects with PowerPoint presentations. One of these project options was to create a survey, administer it, tally the responses, and create a graph to depict the results. The student learned to tally a survey and to create a graph in an online program. Figure 7.5 is taken from one of these projects. This student asked eighth graders about their belief in UFOs, mountain lions, and Bigfoot (in the Gantos novel, a UFO sighting is made by the narrator's crazy uncle).

Another project option was to write a script for and perform an interview with Jack Gantos. Several pairs of students selected this choice. Figure 7.6 shows an image from a creative pair who dubbed in audience applause, wore costumes, and even used makeup to recreate a bloody nose (the narrator of the story is plagued with ceaseless nosebleeds).

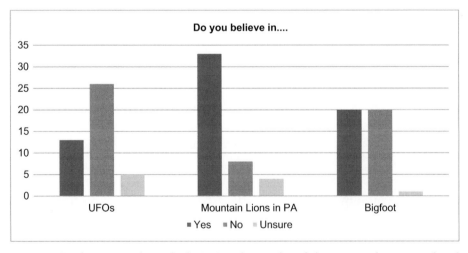

Figure 7.5 Student-created graph depicting the results of the survey they created and implemented to establish what their classmates believed about rural myths and legends

Connecting Content

Figure 7.6 Movie still from a mock interview with *Norvelt* author, Jack Gantos

Figure 7.7 Student project: PA Game Commission brochure

For the outdoor enthusiasts, we had a guest speaker from the Pennsylvania Game Commission. The connected project was to create a brochure explaining the history of the commission and providing information about the hunter safety course. Figure 7.7 shows one of the corresponding projects. This student is also an English language learner who worked closely with his ELL teacher. In the Gantos novel, the narrator goes deer hunting with his father.

End Roadwork

Taking on a cross-curricular project forces many teachers out of their comfort zone because of the unknowns. Teachers, like other learners, have different styles. It can be uncomfortable working with others who do things in unfamiliar ways, but the payoffs for both teachers and students can far outweigh the uneasiness. Quality instruction has defined learning objectives, but the school climate is not a perfect place where events and people never impede the learning process. Often, it is helpful to have another teacher perspective to help navigate the changes and interruptions that seem to naturally occur. It is good for teachers to work and learn together. This improves student and teacher learning; both the professional research and my experience support this. It also contributes to a positive, nurturing school climate that benefits all. Don't be afraid to take risks: push out of your comfort zone.

Another suggestion is to use data to drive instructional choices for collaboration. It addresses real student need and establishes legitimacy with administrators. If a project is focused to address a specific educational need, chances are time, attention, and expertise can meet that need. Teachers need to be reliable, knowledgeable team members who are willing to help when and where there is a need. No single person can know it all; do not be afraid to admit to or address your teaching weaknesses. Working in collaboration is one powerful way to strengthen professional knowledge.

Administrators should encourage teacher collaboration and, more importantly, support it by providing the necessary resources. Time is certainly one of the most vital resources. Teachers need time to discuss, plan, teach, reflect, and evaluate the entire process. They need time to create and evaluate student assessments. Administrators should also take a genuine interest in collaborative teacher projects and get involved in as many stages of the projects as possible. Administrators can celebrate project success and offer constructive feedback in project shortcomings.

To others who provide professional development, I would say do not overlook or underestimate the value of educators' knowledge and expertise. There are innovative teachers in our schools at all levels, from the newly certified to the experienced master teachers. Give teachers a way to identify and learn the refined instructional skills from their peers. Promote the effective teaching that is in place within our schools.

References

Buzzeo, T., & Wilson, S. (2007). Data-driven collaboration in two voices. *Library Media Connection, 26*(2), 20–23.

De Jesus, O. N. (2012). Differentiated instruction: Can differentiated instruction provide success for all learners? *National Teacher Education Journal, 5*(3), 5–11.

Fleischer, C. (2010). *Reading & writing & teens: A parent's guide to adolescent literacy*. National Council Teachers of English. NCTE Stock Number: 39349.

National Center for Literacy Education. (2013). *Remodeling literacy learning: Making room for what works*. Retrieved from www.literacyinlearningrexchange.org

National Council of Teachers of English. (2009). *Writing between the lines—and everywhere else*. Urbana, IL: NCTE.

National Writing Project, & Nagin, C. (2003). *Because writing matters: Improving student writing in our schools*. San Francisco: Jossey-Bass.

Nation's Report Card. (2011). 2011 Writing assessment. U.S. Department of Education, Institute for Education Statistics. National Assessment of Educational Progress.

CHAPTER

8 Connecting Teachers
Teaming up for Essential Vocabulary
Julie Weaver

"Teachers, working together, as evaluators of their impact."

(Hattie, 2013)

Since becoming a National Writing Project Fellow in 2006, I have had the opportunity to work on several teacher-initiated and teacher-directed teams that have had a great impact on our school. They have all centered on science, writing, and vocabulary, and all arose based on struggles we noticed in our students.

A group of the highest-achieving math students in our fourth grade were given a testing challenge in which they had to show how two equations differed. They were stumped, not by the math, but by the word *differed*. Their teachers were baffled. One noted, "We use the word *different* in our class discussions all of the time." On a nonfiction reading assessment, two students asked for assistance on the question, "What factors determine what lives in a river?" Neither student could read the word *determine*. One student puzzled out loud, "I don't know how to deeter mine." Yet, I used the word determine in class with that student often. What was going on here? It was clear that frequency of exposure was not sufficient, as *differ* and *determine* had not become part of our students' working vocabulary.

Then there was Vanessa, who I will never forget. Vanessa always scored 100% on her Friday vocabulary quiz but never seemed to have an understanding of any of the words before or after. I questioned her about her "secret" to success. She did indeed have a "secret." She memorized what the words looked like because she had noticed the weekly quiz answer choices only contained one word from the current week's vocabulary list and the other three choices were from previous weeks. Vanessa had outsmarted the weekly quiz. Sure enough, our reading series had what I consider a fatal flaw, and yet teachers were trained to follow the series with fidelity. In the following weeks, I made up the vocabulary quizzes, and Vanessa struggled to learn the word meaning in order to pass the quizzes. Vanessa was not alone; our class of struggling readers had the learning support teacher and I scrambling to figure out how to help these students master their vocabulary.

A Vocabulary/Writing Study Blossoms

This chapter will chart several successive projects that built on one another in my school and made strong impacts on our teachers and students. So often, when we encounter successes as teachers, we are then met by a change of circumstance that shifts our focus. By identifying the successful elements, we can continue to build on them, even when the situations and contexts change. Programs and texts change, but student learning will always be a priority and a quality goal. In a sense, this chapter is different from the others in that, in places, there are fewer detailed protocols delineated because the related initiatives are included to show how one project springboarded into another.

In the fall of 2008, with funding from the National Writing Project, a group of teachers in our elementary school began collaborating on a project focused on writing to enhance learning in science. A year later, the fourth grade teachers embarked on a follow-up project to integrate vocabulary instruction across the curriculum, with the purpose of increasing student reading comprehension and writing literacy. Since that time, our vocabulary/writing project has waxed, waned, and evolved as teachers have left and joined our staff and a basal reading series was thrust on us. We find ourselves 5 years later returning to fine-tune that vocabulary project and initiating a second writing-in-science collaboration in an effort to incorporate the Common Core Standards. Our school is a public school serving 460 students in grades K–6 in rural north-central Pennsylvania. Fortunately for our school, the Endless Mountain Writing Project (EMWP) was willing to support and fund each of our writing projects.

Since laying that foundation in 2008, we have put together an excellent model for teaming across the curriculum. Our focus has been on improving vocabulary instruction and the quality of student writing, with the primary objective being for students to be able to use written communication to clearly share concepts. Because content-area classrooms are the ideal place for authentic writing, each vocabulary/writing team included content-area teachers. As we take stock of what has come before and are moving ahead with the Common Core, the two greatest challenges for today's teachers have become determining what essential vocabulary to teach and how to help students master and retain that vocabulary so they can express themselves in speaking and in writing. The first step is to determine what is essential.

What Is Essential? The Three Tiers of Vocabulary

What words come to mind when you think of science vocabulary? Which word in the example question, shown in Figure 8.1, would have been assigned as a science vocabulary word in *your* school experience, as a student? Which words are most critical for a student to know to be successful with this question? Is knowing the meaning of the word **species** more essential to understanding what the question asks than the word **frequency** or **decrease**?

A three-tier approach to vocabulary words has been developed and well documented by Beck, McKeown, and Kucan (2008). *Tier one* words are familiar and basic everyday words: words characteristic of spoken language. *Tier two* words are more characteristic of written language. These are the high–utility words for learners across content areas, and are sometimes termed "academic vocabulary." The traditional content-specific vocabulary word is a *tier three* word. *Tier three* words have a narrow application and are not the type of word we would expect students to be able to encounter outside of a discipline or content classroom.

Words such as **frequency** and **decrease** would be identified as *tier two* words by Beck, McKeown, and Kucan (2008) because they are not domain specific but general academic words critical for literacy. Whether it is the **frequency** of bird species, the **frequency** of rolling two sixes on a set of dice, or the **frequency** of homework done correctly, **frequency** is a high utility word. **Decrease** is another *tier two* word at the center of the question. If the meaning of **decrease** is not known, the question cannot be answered without guessing. Beck, McKeown, and Kucan (2008) refer to these tier two words as "high mileage" words; they are words we use frequently when we are writing. It is these *tier two* words that are most important for literacy in content areas that teachers need to focus more direct vocabulary instruction on, especially now that we are expecting students to learn more content at earlier grade levels.

How important is the word **species** to answering the question correctly? The word **species** would be a *tier three* word because **species** is a specific

Month	Sparrows	Finches	Wrens	Warblers	Flycatchers	Cardinals
January	11	2	1	0	0	1
February	12	2	0	0	0	2
March	12	2	3	8	2	1

Figure 8.1 Example science test question for discussing vocabulary selection

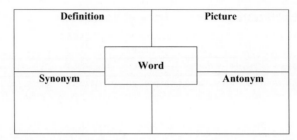

Figure 8.2 Frayer word square template

science concept that would not be encountered by students in their reading outside of science class. These *tier three* words are the vocabulary words that have been traditionally taught in content areas through direct instruction and are words that students must know to meet Common Core State Standards. In my experience, these words are the ones students learn fairly easily at the elementary level: matter, solid, liquid, and gas. Content-area teachers need to extend their vocabulary instruction to include the *tier two* words that are so critical to content literacy. These are words I assumed my students would know, such as "differ" and "determine."

A definition of a word is not enough to move students from recognition to ownership. Frayer word squares for vocabulary include a student-friendly definition of the concept word, an example of the word done as a drawing, a synonym, and an antonym (see Figure 8.2). Including synonyms and antonyms is important so students are able to identify what the concept word is and what it is not (Frayer, Frederick, & Klausmeier, 1969).

Learning to identify what words are essential for literacy in content areas, devoting time for their direct instruction, and promoting student mastery is crucial to reach the objective of clear written communication of ideas. The next step is to move our students' vocabulary from recognition words to words of expression.

From Recognition to Expressive

Expert writers construct meaning as they write. This process is often called "writing to learn." "Teachers can use writing as a way to encourage thinking because it provides students with time to discover what it is they think, and not just to record their thoughts" (Fisher & Frey, 2007, p. 5). Knowing the content is only the first step. Giving students the time and opportunity to write in content-area classes is essential. If we want students to be critical thinkers, they must be able to communicate in the language of content areas.

Frequent opportunities to use words are essential to get students to move to full ownership from simple recognition of those words (Coskie & Davis, 2009). Students who gain ownership of the words that characterize written language will become powerful writers who can effectively express themselves.

Words should be prominently displayed in the classroom on word walls or in word banks where students can easily find them when writing. Coskie and Davis (2009) advocate for word walls that sort the content (tier three) words from the high utility (tier two) words. Then teachers can model the organization and use of words on the word wall in their speaking and teaching. Fisher and Frey (2007) recommend that teachers model and think aloud as they demonstrate how to incorporate new vocabulary in content-area writing. Guided practice must follow modeling to allow the shift in responsibility from the teacher to the students. Science lends itself to collaborative learning in which the students who have experimented together can then work together to revise writing supported by word walls. This shared experience without the teacher gives students the opportunity to be both the writer/speaker and the listener (Fisher & Frey, 2007).

The more word-aware we can make our students, the more likely they will be to use the words from the wall in their writing and speaking. Composing sentences in science is a powerful learning process and can be greatly enhanced if we can help students use the language of science (Toppings & McManus, 2002). This language is critical in developing scientific reasoning and conceptual understanding. Student ownership of vocabulary occurs when students choose to use their vocabulary words to express themselves in writing throughout the year and across the curriculum. Beck, McKeown, and Kucan (2008) find frequent and varied encounters that extend beyond the week the words are learned are crucial to developing a rich knowledge of words that will stay in memory and be used across content areas. Students must write to learn.

EUREKA! An In-Service Model for Elementary Writing in Science, 2008–2009

The theme of the teacher development series our Writing Project (WP) site sponsored in 2008 was "Writing to enhance learning in science." The series was titled "EUREKA" as an Archimedes-referenced acronym for "Educators Unleashing Experience, Knowledge & Applications."

EUREKA was a group that explored science learning and thinking through writing. The group met on the fourth Wednesday of each month, right after school, for 1 hour, for a total of 5 hours/sessions. Based on the National Writing Project model of teacher development in which teachers teach teachers, the workshops were led by five teacher consultants (TCs) who had completed an invitational WP Summer Institute. The group met in the school library from 3:30 to 4:30, and attendance was open for all faculty. Each participant received a copy of a reference book titled *ScienceSaurus* (Great Source Education Group, 2006) for the sessions, to use as the source text on which to implement the teaching strategies. This text was selected by the Writing Project director, based on her previous experiences with the publisher's formatting and her work with content-area reading and writing.

I was given a handful of copies of the text to use as a recruiting tool for the EUREKA sessions, and the WP printed out fliers that were placed into teachers' mailboxes (see Appendix F). At the completion of the EUREKA series, teachers who had participated in the majority of them were to receive a full class set of the *ScienceSaurus* texts, with the volume that was most appropriate for the grade level they were teaching. Using *ScienceSaurus* as a source text gave the participants hands-on training with the actual teaching strategies, helped them become acquainted with a target text, and generated actual examples that they could use to model the strategies with their students.

Format for the EUREKA Sessions

At each session, an EMWP fellow modeled a specific, expository, science-related writing strategy in the first 10–15 minutes. Presentations were clear, upbeat, and informed by each presenter's classroom experience with their own students. Completed samples made by students were made available for review. Then, participants used the strategy in small groups using a section of the *ScienceSaurus* text as their content for 30 minutes. Each of the activities involved extensive writing and was focused on designing an activity that was grade appropriate and could be taken back to the classroom. In the final 15 minutes, each participant discussed how he or she specifically could use the strategy in his or her classroom. Sessions were spaced a month apart, which provided ample time for teachers to take the writing strategy back to their classrooms and try it with their own students.

At each workshop, participants were given a two-page handout. The first page outlined the basics of the strategy, which included mini-books, "stop and jot," science notebooks, observing and predicting, and place-based writing. A clear basis in research was reflected on the second page of the handout, which contained sources directly relating to the topic. Sources were abstracted and fully cited so that participants could find the entire work if they wished. A total of 11 teachers representing grades K–5 participated in the workshop. The workshop was well received: exit survey scores all were 4.75 or higher out of a total of 5.

My Life as a Point Person and Sticky Note

In the following fall (2009), I was designated as a point person at the school to check in on the participants several times a month. My task was to see how teachers were using the strategies and the text books in conjunction with writing over the course of the following year. As the point person, I sometimes felt like a human sticky note, circulating with the words, "writing, science, and EUREKA" written in bold face print! However, I never felt that my visits were an imposition. In fact, most teachers were excited to talk about and show off the successes they were having using writing strategies and the *ScienceSaurus* text. I thoroughly enjoyed my visits to other classrooms and only wish I had more time to observe and interact with the students while using the strategies. Probably one of the greatest benefits of having a point person in the building was the frequent informal discussions about writing and science that occurred throughout the year in the building. Often, these discussions involved faculty that were not involved in the EUREKA project, which was a bonus. Listening to teachers excited about writing and science can be contagious, and did result in shared ideas beyond the workshop participants.

Positive and Lasting Results

A survey of the teachers who participated in the workshop shows that the strategies were very well received. In addition, the same survey showed that each of the teachers placed great value on writing in science and using writing activities combined with the *ScienceSaurus* text to impact student learning. All of the teachers rated writing in science to have great value (see Figure 8.3).

We had not surveyed the teachers prior to our EUREKA workshop on the value of writing to learn science, nor did we think to survey the students on their opinion. In hindsight, I wish we had the data; however, there is no doubt that the amount of writing and importance of writing in science increased in our school as a direct result of this work.

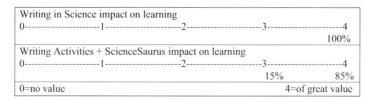

Figure 8.3 EUREKA participants rate writing in science (April 2009)

How much does writing help you learn science?

Grade	None	Somewhat	A lot
3	6	21	25
4	2	25	31
5	1	16	34
6	1	24	35
Total %	5%	38%	57%

Figure 8.4 September 2013 student survey

Fast forward to September 2013, when a group composed of science teachers from grades 3–6 teamed up to focus on writing in science. This time, the students were surveyed; all third to sixth grade students (221 total) were asked their opinion of the value of writing to learn science. We were quite surprised at the data shown in Figure 8.4 because of the reluctance perceived by teachers when students are asked to write.

Our students know that they learn better when they write. I believe this is a testament to the value of the EUREKA workshop held in 2008–2009. We appear to be right on board with Common Core, as the two most significant shifts in these standards is the placement of writing in content areas and the balance among narrative, informational, and argument in writing.

Branching Off to Focus on Vocabulary to Improve Writing

Toward the close of the EUREKA sessions in the spring of 2009, a team of teachers proposed to further improve writing across the curriculum, specifically at the fourth grade level. The teachers developed a plan to help the students acquire an integrated working vocabulary that would enrich writing across the curriculum. EMWP was approached and agreed to fund the project. The goal was to improve the effectiveness of our writing and reading instruction by collaborating as a grade level team on vocabulary. Our plan included four fourth grade teachers working together in the way we teach vocabulary, as well as focusing on the actual words we teach. We used index cards color coded by subject on which the students made Frayer word squares.

The students collected the cards and kept them on a ring, adding to them as the year went on. As the students moved among the subject areas, they would carry this Working Writing Vocabulary card ring with them. When students had to write in any class, they would have their vocabulary words at their fingertips. We predicted this would enrich both writing and reading

Encounter—introduce words in context, direct instruction, picture–word associations, Frayer word squares
Word bank—visible in classroom, allows frequent encounters with the words
Model/Practice—speaking and writing, move words from recognition to ownership
Writing—scaffolded writing instruction to shift the responsibility to the students

Figure 8.5 Four steps to developing vocabulary in content areas

comprehension across the curriculum and allow students to really master their vocabulary words. This project was used in conjunction with the Harcourt *StoryTown* reading series' robust vocabulary. In addition, each of the four teachers set up an integrated word wall in their classrooms from all the subject areas, leaving the previous words up, so by the end of the year, all the vocabulary words would be posted in all classrooms.

In the fall of 2009, our team of fourth grade teachers began a four-step program to focus on the quality of student writing in the content area. This process is outlined in Figure 8.5.

We provided students with opportunities to write approximately once a week—usually, an on-demand written response to text or content. Each writing task involved modeling, followed by guided practice.

We began this project in September 2008. Measuring the effectiveness of the vocabulary project was based on *4Sight* testing data, as well as anecdotal observations by the teachers. *4Sight* is a series of tests that are aligned to our state's academic standards, and are intended to measure progress from test to test over the course of the school year. *4Sight* data was collected four times throughout the project, with a baseline test given in September and the final test given in late May.

Rough Spots

Posting all the vocabulary words did not work as well as we had planned. Space was limited, so we focused only on the robust vocabulary from the reading series with the vocabulary from our own subject area. Not only was the vocabulary there for the students to use but, also, we found that as teachers, we were much more inclined to use the words from the wall in our everyday teaching and conversation. This posting of words definitely increased the students' exposure to the words, not just on the week that the words were learned but throughout the year.

Several of our learning support students had very large writing and were not able to write on the index cards. The learning support teachers developed a template that they would copy onto card stock paper to accommodate these students. These cards were large and bulky and not as easily carried on a ring, so the students used zip lock bags.

By the last quarter of the year, many of the zip lock bags were ripping and cards were tearing loose from rings and getting lost. The positive side of this is that the students were using the cards so much that they were getting ragged; on the negative side, they were losing cards. The rings themselves were also showing signs of wear; many rings would no longer close properly.

Teachers found that giving extra points for using vocabulary words in writing or speaking was an excellent incentive and led to students looking for and finding vocabulary words in their reading, as well. Tickets were given when a vocabulary word was used by a student or found by a student. Students accumulated tickets to earn erasers, grippers, pencils, or lunch with the teacher.

Testing Positive

There is no question that this vocabulary project increased the working vocabulary of our students. We saw it in their writing, we heard it in their conversation, and it was reflected in their *4Sight* test scores. At the start of the project in September, only 45% of our students were proficient on *4Sight* tests, but by the end of May, this percentage had increased 42% to an overall percentage of 87. These same students at the end of their third grade year tested 70% proficient on the 2007/2008 *4Sight* tests. Grades 3, 5, and 6 all used the same Harcourt *StoryTown* reading series for the first time this year, which included the robust vocabulary instruction. However, the fourth grade was the only grade level that participated in the vocabulary card project using the Frayer method for learning the words. Figure 8.6 shows that the improvement at the fourth grade level was twice that of any other grade level.

Grade level	Percentage of Students Proficient—September	Percentage of Students Proficient—May	Net Change
3	38%	60%	+22%
4	45%	87%	+45%
5	52%	70%	+18%
6	57%	61%	+4%

Figure 8.6 Comparison of grade 3–6. PA reading scaled score proficiencies

Examples of Student Writing

The work of three students was selected to show the impact of the vocabulary/writing project on writing. Students from three of the PSSA reporting categories were used, as indicated in the parentheses below. A September writing sample is provided for each of the three students, followed by a writing sample taken later in the year. Robust vocabulary words are italicized. The September samples tell mostly facts with few descriptive words. When descriptive words are used, they are mostly tier one words: fun, long, sharp, brown, nice, boring, tired, and cool. The writing improves significantly when the robust vocabulary words are added.

Student A in September Writing Sample (Below Basic)

We were in my dad's car for a long time. Me, Dedria all sat in the van. I was mad because it was boring. We were going on vacation to north carolina. When we got there we went to Knights Inn. We went to lunch, then went swimming in the nice cool water. Then we fell into bed.

Student A in November, after 3 Months of Robust Vocabulary Instruction (Basic)

Our class went on a field trip to L.H. State Park. I was so excited to get to the lookout. The view was *stunning!* I could see the *sparkling* river. It was beautiful. I was trying to get a better look so I stepped upon the wooden fence and leaned over. All the students were *jostling* each other and I slipped and fell. "help." I cried. I was rolling fast down the hill! I could see *clusters* of trees rushing past. I *swerved* and tried not to hit a tree. I *cringed* as I saw the drop off and I fell 100 feet. I was falling as calm as a feather. All of a sudden I found myself snuggled in an eagles nest. I was so *comfortable* I fell asleep.

Student B in September Writing Sample (Basic)

I(t) was our 2nd game in the season. Me, the team and our coaches were so excited! I was the first one to make a goal. Then my best friend Darby got the ball and made a goal. The score was 2–0 and we were winning the game! Then they made a goal so we were still winning but they were catching up. It was break time. Me and the whole team was sweating and tired.

Student B in June (Proficient)

As we walked and walked down the moist cave it got darker and creepier. I felt a little *queasy* at first then I was OK. I tried to dodge the *stalactites.* The Crystal lake was *sparkling* and glowing. Bill, our tour guide showed us and talked to us about the wedding chapel and how the imprint of a wedding cake got in the wall. You have to be very *flexible* to fit through the cave. And the coolest thing was we were all doing this one hundred feet underground! How awesome is that?

Student C in September Writing Sample (Proficient)

One day in August I went to my grandparents' house. I played with the lively brown dog Jack. It was hot and sticky that day so I was wearing my shorts. My fun aunt Melissa came out of the house and said that we were going for a walk in the woods. We started walking. When we got to the woods I wished that I had worn my jeans because there were a lot of sharp picker bushes.

Student C in May (Proficient)

My fourth grade went on a field trip April 25th to Harrisburg, PA. My favorite part (was) hiking through a *massive* cave with *magnificent* rock form(ation)s. This cave was Indian Echo Caverns. After the cave we went to the State Museum. There was a *colossal* statue of William Penn. There was also long houses and statues of Indians. Last we went to the Capitol of Pennsylvania. I was *stunned,* the capitol was really *fancy.*

Aligning with the Common Core Standards

A close look into the Common Core Standards reaffirmed our team's belief that we were on the correct path in our integrated vocabulary/writing program. The research repeatedly showed that vocabulary is foundational for literacy and, not surprisingly, we find vocabulary and writing at the core of the new Common Core Standards. Vocabulary in the Common Core Standards focuses on the students' ability to retain and use academic and general academic vocabulary to improve literacy across all content. Writing is viewed as "a key means of asserting and defending claims, showing what they (students) know about a subject, and conveying what they have experienced, imagined, thought and felt." (W.CCR)

As we began the 2013 school year, we renewed our purpose to create word-conscious classrooms that focused on both vocabulary instruction and quality of writing with the primary objective of clear written communication of ideas. Figure 8.7 juxtaposes our four-step program with Silver, Dewing, and Perini's (2012) matrix of vocabulary's CODE from their work, the *Core Six*.

The two sides of the chart mirror each other in developing strategies to master essential vocabulary, which, in turn, improves literacy across the curriculum and will ultimately develop higher order thinking skills through writing. Common Core State Standards (CCSS) make it clear that to make students

Four Steps to Developing Vocabulary in Content Areas	Common Core Matrix of Vocabulary's CODE
Encounter—introduce words in context, direct instruction, picture–word associations, Frayer word squares	Connect—forming a strong connection with initial contact
Word bank—visible in classroom, allows frequent encounters with the words	Organize—how terms are related and how they fit together in a bigger context
Model/Practice—speaking and writing, critical to move words from recognition to ownership	Deep-process—multiple forms of representation, using thinking strategies to understand deeply
Writing—scaffolded writing instruction to shift the responsibility to the students	Exercise—engaging students in meaningful practice and committing words to long-term memory

Figure 8.7 Aligning vocabulary with Common Core

career- and college-ready, teachers must incorporate writing "for a range of tasks, purposes and audiences." (W.CCR.10)

> CCSS.ELA–Literacy.RI.4.4: Determine the meaning of general academic and domain-specific words or phrases in a text relevant to a *grade 4 topic or subject area.*
> CCSS.ELA–Literacy.W.4.1: Write opinion pieces on topics or texts, supporting a point of view with reasons and information.
> CCSS.ELA–Literacy.W.4.2: Write informative/explanatory texts to examine a topic and convey ideas and information clearly.
> CCSS.ELA–Literacy.W.4.10: Write routinely over extended time frames (time for research, reflection, and revision) and shorter time frames (a single sitting or a day or two) for a range of discipline-specific tasks, purposes, and audiences.

In Alignment: Four Adjustments

Essential Vocabulary

We had the most success with the robust vocabulary from the reading series across the curriculum because the robust vocabulary was identified for the teachers to use. However, after a bit of research into the three tiers of vocabulary, we determined that we had been focusing mostly on the tier three words, not the general academic or high utility words for writing. We, as teachers, needed to choose our essential vocabulary, rather than letting the basal series determine our vocabulary for us. This change predated the Common Core Standards but proved to be in alignment with the Common Core.

Where the students recorded their vocabulary word squares was another small change we made. After much discussion about how to collect vocabulary, we decided to ask the students. Their solution to the ragged and lost index cards was to use a spiral notebook with 100 pages that could be split into four sections per page, which would allow 400 words to be collected throughout the year.

Words Introduced in Context

We also noticed that when faced with a list of eight or more words to define, our students would focus only on getting the vocabulary done. When we changed course and gave two or three words a day, the students focused on the words rather than the task. Introducing fewer words at a time was especially important for the struggling readers. This did not fit the basal reader schedule of words presented on Monday, tested on Friday, but after 20 years of teaching, I followed my instincts and believed in formative assessments more than the basal reader schedule. Now, students encounter each vocabulary word where and when it is most appropriate. Silver, Dewing, and Perini (2012) emphasize the importance of a strong initial connection with terms in their vocabulary CODE matrix.

Now, introduction of words happens in context, followed by direct instruction. For example, we were recently working on a unit in science on natural resources. The students played a game from Project Learning Tree called "Greed vs. Need." The object of the game is to survive by taking popcorn from a shared renewable resource supply. After playing the first set of rounds, many groups had depleted their supply, while other groups had resources remaining. This is when the word **conserve** was first introduced. The groups that conserved their resource survived longer than those that did not. We stopped to define the word, discuss examples, and draw pictures using a modified Frayer word square. An example of a student vocabulary notebook showing the word **conserve** is shown in Figure 8.8.

Since my encounter with students stumped by the word **differ**, I started including the endings that can be added to the vocabulary word (e.g., conserve, conserved, conserving, conservation, and conservationist), as I want my fourth graders to recognize all forms of the word. Students place words in a vocabulary notebook that travels with the student to each class every day, and words are posted on word walls in classrooms, as they are collected.

After building the word square for the word conserve, the students played the Greed vs. Need game again to see if the students learned to conserve their renewable resource supply. The students quickly learned to take only what they needed to survive. In the third set of rounds, the students gave an example of how

Connecting Teachers

Figure 8.8 Student vocabulary notebook

they could conserve a renewable resource, as well as how the resource is renewed (previous vocabulary words) in real life using the words conserve, resource, and renewed. This is the model/practice or deep-processing step, critical to developing a conceptual understanding and student ownership. One word was added to the vocabulary notebook that day in science; however, several words learned on previous days were reviewed. On the same day, students collected vocabulary from other content areas, as well, one of which happened to be **realistic**—a word that generated a discussion of how realistic our renewable resource game was.

Word Walls become a Priority

Posting all the vocabulary words did not work as well as we had planned back in 2009. Space was limited, so we focused only on the robust vocabulary from the reading series with the vocabulary from our own subject areas. Since then, we have made the word wall a priority. The word wall encourages both the students and the teacher to use the words in speaking and writing. When a new unit is introduced, the content words may change but the high utility or tier two words should remain. In our fourth grade, each teacher has a word wall on which not only their content-specific words are posted, but any vocabulary words from the other classes that we feel we can use in our classrooms. Words are organized and visible. I have four sections of words at present: Science, Math and Reading Content, High Use, and Prefixes/Suffixes. A quick glance at the word wall, and I can incorporate a word from another

Figure 8.9 Science classroom word wall

class, as can a student. This posting of words definitely increases the students' exposure to the words, not just on the week that the words were learned, but throughout the year. See Figure 8.9 for an example from my classroom.

As students work in class on scientific investigations, they record information in their notebooks using their own expressive language. At the beginning of the year, this writing tends to be non-scientific and lacking in science vocabulary. Borrowing these student entries is an opportune time for the teacher to model how to rewrite or self-edit to improve the scientific language using the word bank. I use sticky strips to display words so they can easily be moved and regrouped when needed.

It is not long into the school year when I no longer am the one suggesting the changes; students get very adept at using words from the wall to improve their own writing, as well as their classmates'. A student recently recorded the observation during a lab activity, "As salt went up more colors of crayons floated." As the sentence was shared with the class, a classmate took words from the word wall to improve the sentence to "As the *amount* of salt *increased* more colors of crayons floated." *Amount* and *increased* were high utility words from the word wall.

As the year goes on, with the words visible on the classroom wall, in the ideal situation, students would chose to use the words on their own in their notebooks, moving the words to their expressive vocabulary as they write to learn.

Daily Writing in Content

Each and every day, our students write in their classes. In their argument for why teachers need to write to learn across the curriculum to address the Common Core, Silver, Dewing, and Perini, (2012) state, "Writing is as flexible and inexhaustible as language itself, meaning that no single classroom technique or set of implementation steps can effectively capture its dynamic power" (p. 52). Short quick-writes about what students learned provides formative assessment about how well they have grasped the content. Often, I ask students to write using certain words from the word wall, or I may give them a selection that I would like them to choose from. Here, the students can exercise their expressive language by making meaning through writing. A quick, over-the-shoulder glance gives me an accurate picture of how well a student has mastered the vocabulary. In the renewable resource example described previously, to wrap up the activity, students were asked to write what they learned from the Greed vs. Need game with the following suggested words to use in their writing: conserve, renewable, resource, and supply.

I often begin class with a quick-write, in which students must predict or explain background knowledge. These written responses give me valuable formative information and help guide my instruction. At least once a week, I ask for a longer writing assignment, an argument, or an informative piece. This writing requires students to organize their thoughts and use evidence from their reading or lab work to support their ideas. See Figures 8.10 and 8.12 for an example of a graphic organizer and the resulting essay on how weathering and erosion shape the land.

"Keep It or Junk It"

Amazing things happen when students are the ones to determine which words are essential. One technique that our team has started using with great success is the "Keep it or Junk It" student-led lesson (Brouhard, 2012). Students individually read a passage and highlight what they consider to be words essential to answering a focus question. Students get together in groups to compare their essential words and decide as a group whether they should "keep" or "junk" the words. Groups come up with a list of essential words to propose to the class. Student groups propose their words to the class one at a time and everyone must vote with their fingers: 1 = keep it, 2 = junk it, 3 = cloud it (not sure). A student who would like to keep the word is called on to argue for keeping the

Julie Weaver

Beginning What information am I explaining?	Middle What are the key parts of my explanation?		End Close the writing
How can I introduce my topic clearly?	Magic 3: Key details	How will I develop each detail to inform or explain the topic?	How will I summarize my topic?
①River ②carve ③deposit ④sidiments ⑤delta ⑥land Rivers carve land, and deposit sediments	1. Rainstorm	A rainstorm rains on a watershed and creates a runoff that takes the water to the river.	These are the the two ways that a river shapes land.
	2. Carve	A river carves valleys and canyons over time and the river erodes sediments	
	3. deposit	When the river deposites sediments the river creates deltas downstream.	

Focus question: How does a river system work to change the shape of the land surface?

Figure 8.10 3x3 writing organizer

word based on the focus question. A second student is called on who voted to junk the word to argue why the word should be junked. The class votes again after hearing both arguments and the students in charge must decide to keep or junk the word based on how essential the word is to the focus question. This strategy is all about students finding evidence and being able to argue based on that evidence—all Common Core Standard skills. When a student has a solid argument for the value of a word in answering a focus question, you can be sure they have a deep understanding of the word. Once the class has determined the words essential to answering the focus question, the next step is for students to answer the focus question in writing using the words they voted to keep.

Recently, I used this strategy on a passage describing how weathering and erosion shape the land. The focus question is in the upper left-hand corner of Figure 8.10.

The words the class voted to keep are on the right-hand side of the graphic organizer that students used to organize their writing. In this case, the students voted on nine essential words. A few words were added in pencil at the beginning of class as we completed the "Keep It or Junk It" activity. I also included the five words that the students put in the cloud (circled words) because they

Connecting Teachers

1 word	2 words	3 words	4 words	5 words	6 words	7 words	8 words	9 words	10 words
–	–	–	–	–	9%	5%	23%	43%	19%

Figure 8.11 Percentage of students using essential vocabulary correctly in writing

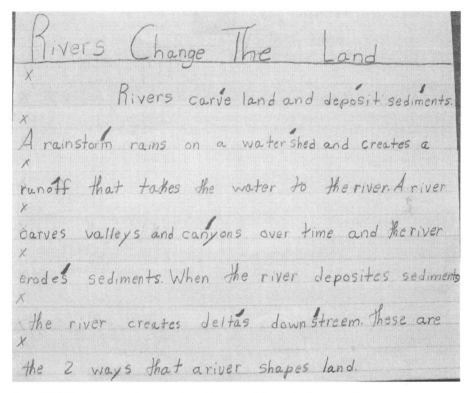

Figure 8.12 Student writing sample with essential vocabulary words

were unsure of how essential these words were, and so they were available if they choose to use them. Figure 8.11 shows how often students used the essential words in their writing.

All students used at least six of the essential vocabulary words. The majority (85%) of students used 8–10 of the nine essential words correctly in their writing. Only 19% of the students used additional words from the cloud. Figure 8.12 shows an example of the writing that goes along with this student's graphic organizer.

The accent marks show each essential word that was used correctly. When students are responsible for identifying the essential words, they are more likely to use those words in their writing.

115

Assessing Student Use of Vocabulary

Assessment of student learning must go beyond measuring recognition of words to measuring expressive use of vocabulary words in writing. Any study of student growth in expressive vocabulary must cover a long enough period of time to track potential effects of vocabulary instruction on quality of writing (Beck, McKeown, & Kucan, 2008). Using a science notebook, in which students do all their writing about science, provides a longitudinal record of how a student's writing has progressed throughout the year. If writing in science is thinking on paper, then by reading a student's notebook, we should get a view into student thoughts about concepts, based on their expressive language and their word choices.

Counting and tracking the correct use of vocabulary words to express ideas can be done effectively through use of a rubric when students complete the on-demand style of writing assessed in standardized tests, as shown in Figure 8.13.

Through modeling and scaffolding, students are taught to highlight key words from the question, as well as the text, to use in their writing. Restating the question is the first step they are taught through modeling, followed by scaffolding when writing a response. Using rubrics as a guide for writing reminds the students to use the vocabulary from the word wall. Often, the assignment and/or rubric will include a suggested word bank. Recently, I randomly distributed a writing assignment to 50 students, in which half of the rubrics had a word bank and the other half did not. Students who were given a word bank used more vocabulary words than those who were not given a word bank, as shown in Figure 8.14.

	Not Present 0	Correct and Complete = 2	Uses Evidence 2	Word-wall Vocabulary 2	Total Possible 6
Concluding Statement					

Figure 8.13 Assessment rubric—conclusion

Writing Assignment on Endangered Species	Average Target Science Vocabulary Words Used
With word bank (9 words)	5
Without word bank	3

Figure 8.14 Comparison of writing with/without word bank

I was happy to see that those without the word bank still did use an average of 30% of the target science words. I shared this data with the students and they were quite interested in the results. In keeping with a word-conscious classroom, involving students in the techniques I am using to help them become more expressive writers is important, as well.

Measuring Success

Our school building received a High Performing School Honor from the state of Pennsylvania in December 2013. To receive this distinction, a school has to be in the top 98 out of the 1,008 Title 1 schools. In the 23 years since I joined the faculty at Miller Elementary School, I have seen the evolution from teachers working behind closed doors to teacher-initiated collaborations that have affected real change in the way our students learn and achieve. As delineated in this chapter, professional development and teacher collaboration can be incredibly effective when the efforts are aligned and refined over time, and the lessons we learn as teachers have definite, positive impact on our students.

References

Beck, I. L., McKeown, M. G., & Kucan, L. (2008). *Creating robust vocabulary: Frequently asked questions and extended examples.* New York: The Guilford Press.

Brouhard, J. (2012). *Keep it or junk it.* Videocast retrieved from www.teaching channel.org/videos/student-run-lesson

Coskie, T. L, and Davis, K. J. (2009). Word wall work: Supporting science talk. *Science and Children, 46*(8) 56–58.

Fisher, D., & Frey, N. (2007). *Scaffolded writing instruction: Teaching with a gradual-release framework.* New York: Scholastic.

Frayer, D., Frederick, W. C., & Klausmeier, H. J. (1969). *A schema for testing the level of cognitive mastery.* Madison, WI: Wisconsin Center for Education Research.

Great Source Education Group. (2006). *ScienceSaurus: A student handbook.* Boston, MA: Houghton-Mifflin Publishing.

Hattie, J. (2013). Why are so many of our teachers and schools so successful? *TEDx Norrköping: Learning from past when designing the future.* Video presentation retrieved from www.ted.com/tedx/events/7581

Silver, H. F., Dewing, R. T., & Perini, M. J. (2012). *The core six essential strategies for achieving excellence with the common core.* Alexandria, VA: ASCD.

Toppings, D., & McManus, R. (2002). *Real reading, real writing: Content area strategies.* Portsmouth, NH: Heinemann.

CHAPTER

Conclusion: Let There Be Light
Where Will You Connect?

Nanci Werner-Burke

What would a student's day and life look like in a setting where he or she encountered and became a part of all of these initiatives? How much more effective could teachers be if they were able to work openly and creatively with the support of parents, students, and colleagues alike? This text details initiatives that took effort, planning, and long-term diligence, not just to undertake, but to see through and then commit to writing about the results. It is our hope that our endings will provide for new beginnings, both for the teachers whose work is documented here (our work is never really done!) and for the educators and community members who are our readers.

What can you use from this collection of action research that can build capacity for learning in your school? Begin by asking what resources and organizations are already in place or available to help communicate with parents and families about how education has changed since they were in school, and how they can be a part of preparing their children to be successful in and beyond school. How can you plan and implement ways to connect with students outside of your classroom? What are other teachers doing already along these lines? How well do teachers communicate in your building and district, in terms of connecting their content and curriculum, and working together to choose the right materials and strategies for students? By asking these questions, you may find that there are already practices in place, and all that is needed is to get involved and bring your teaching toolkit.

Chances are that, given the areas identified in this book and on your wish list, there are ones that still need attention or have no resources or support systems in place. Once you have found them, your task will start to become clear. Open your classroom door and step into a place where you can take a different type of action, one that will have positive and lasting impact on your students and their world.

The contributors welcome your questions and comments, and can be contacted through the Endless Mountains Writing Project (EMWP). The EMWP can be contacted through the National Writing Project (www.nwp.org), which is a grant-funded, national network of teacher leaders devoted to writing-related professional development efforts across the nation. Visit the NWP online if you are interested in finding out more of what the site nearest you is offering in terms of resources and professional development.

In keeping with our emphasis on connections and outreach, the proceeds from this text are being donated to the Mansfield Free Public Library in Mansfield, Pennsylvania. Celebrating more than 100 years in existence, the library has long been a beacon of literacy in our community, where young and old alike gather to read, play, and grow. It is one of the remaining Carnegie Libraries, started with funding from industrialist Andrew Carnegie, and it seems fitting to close with one of his quotes, which reflects the leadership and initiative of the teachers in this volume. Carnegie (1889) believed in giving to the "industrious and ambitious; not those who need everything done for them, but those who, being most anxious and able to help themselves, deserve and will be benefited by help from others." It is in that spirit that we have undertaken these projects and turn the results over to you, to help you as we have helped ourselves to reach our students.

Reference

Carnegie, A. (1889). The best fields for philanthropy. *The North American Review, 149*(397), 682–698. Retrieved from http://cdl.library.cornell.edu/

Appendices

APPENDIX A

In November Newsletter

Family Literacy Children's Book Club

Book Choice

When choosing a book to read, you want to find a story that is not too easy or too hard for your child to understand. A simple method to help them choose is called the **Five Finger Rule**.

Follow these easy steps to help you and your child find books at their level:

1. Open a book to the middle.
2. Choose a full page of words.
3. Read the page.
4. Hold up a finger each time you come to a word you don't know or understand.

- If you hold up just your thumb: Thumbs Up! You knew all but one word. This book will be pretty easy for you.
- If you hold up 2 fingers: "L" stands for learning. You might need some help but it will be a good learning book for you.
- If you hold up 3 fingers: "W" is for warning. You can read this book, but it is a warning that it might be frustrating and you may not enjoy it.
- If you hold up 4 or 5 fingers: this is the STOP signal. This would be a good book to stop reading by yourself and read with someone else.

K-1st Grades

In November
by Cynthia Rylant

October/November 2012

"The more books children own, the more they read, and the more comfortable they feel choosing books away from home."

—Donalyn Miller

The Book Whisperer

"Surrounding children with books — in libraries, classrooms, and at home - positively affects reading interest and achievement."

Read Alouds

"Reading aloud is one of the most important things parents and teachers can do with children. Reading aloud builds many important foundational skills, introduces vocabulary, provides a model of fluent, expressive reading, and helps children recognize what reading for pleasure is all about."

(www.readingrockets.org)

- For our story, sit down and take 15 minutes to read aloud *In November*. After you have read the story multiple times, have your child pick a favorite page or favorite line to read aloud to you.

Appendix A

Repetition in Reading

"Repetition makes books predictable, and young readers love knowing what comes next. Find books with repeated phrases and short rhyming poems." A few favorite books are:

- *Alexander and the Terrible, Horrible, No Good, Very Bad Day* by Judith Viorst
- *Brown Bear, Brown Bear, What Do You See?* by Bill Martin Jr.
- *Horton Hatches the Egg* by Dr. Seuss
- *The Little Engine That Could* by Watty Piper

(www.readingrockets.org).

In November contains the repetition of "In November" to start off each page. Take a picture walk through the story. Have your child use the pictures on the page to describe what they think is happening "In November". Use the activity sheet attached to go through the other eleven months to match up what happens throughout the year.

Discussion Questions– *In November*

During reading or after reading is a great time to ask questions about the story. This helps to improve comprehension. Here are some questions to discuss the story:

1. How were the leafless trees standing?
2. How did the birds look?
3. What do animals do in November?
4. What color was the November food smell? How can smell be a color?
5. What did the people give thanks for?

"In November, the Earth is growing quiet. It is making its bed, a winter bed for small flowers and creatures. The bed is white and silent, and much life can hide beneath its blanket."

Activities– *In November*

Use the connections down below to build knowledge, write, and get outside with your reader:

- Describe what Thanksgiving was like when you were a child. Use your five senses: touch, taste, see, smell, and hear.
- Have your child plan what they would like to have for a Thanksgiving meal. Use the attached menu to write down their ideas.
- Take a walk outside looking for the signs of winter mentioned in the story, *In November*.
- Match up what happens in the twelve months throughout the year using the attached pictures and squares.

More Books...

For further reading of stories like *In November,* check out:

- *The Relative Came* by Cynthia Rylant
- *Night in the Country* by Cynthia Rylant
- *Leaf Man* by Lois Ehlert
- *Over the River and Through the Wood* by Lydia Maria Child

APPENDIX B

Animalia Newsletter

Family Literacy Children's Book Club

Next Meeting

February 4, 2013

5:30–6:30 P.M.

RB Walter Elementary School Library

Meet for food, fun, and the wonderful world of children's books!

Kids Activities Included

K–1st Grades

Animalia
by Graeme Base

December/January
2012–2013

"Reading aloud with children is known to be the single most important activity for building the knowledge and skills they will eventually require for learning to read." —Marilyn Jager Adams

Just for Fun

The incentive to read is different for every child. Play is a powerful way to get young children to learn. Every time you play, sing, or read with young children, they are learning about language. Song and rhyme are going to be part of our adventure while reading *Animalia*.

"Within the pages of this book
You may discover, if you look
Beyond the spell of written words,
A hidden land of beasts and birds.
For many things are 'of a kind,'
And those with keenest eyes will find
A thousand things, or maybe more—
It's up to you to keep the score."

—Graeme Base

Appendix B

World of Words

Here are a few ways to create a home rich in words.

What you'll need:
- Paper
- Pencils, crayons, markers
- Glue
- Newspapers, magazines
- Safety scissors

What to do:
- Hang posters of the alphabet on the bedroom walls or make an alphabet poster with your child. Print the letters in large type. Capital letters are usually easier for young children to learn first.
- Label the things in your child's pictures. If your child draws a picture of a house, label it with "This is a house." and put it on the refrigerator.

- Have your child watch you write when you make a shopping list or a "what to do" list. Say the words aloud and carefully print each letter.
- Let your child make lists, too. Help your child form the letters and spell the words.
- Look at newspapers and magazines with your child. Find an interesting picture and show it to your child as you read the caption aloud.
- Create a scrapbook. Cut out pictures of people and places and label them.

By exposing your child to words and letters often, your child will begin to recognize the shapes of letters. The world of words will become friendly.

(Idea from: www.readingrockets.org)

Discussion Questions– *Animalia*

During reading or after reading is a great time to ask questions about the story. This helps to improve comprehension. Here are some questions to discuss with the story:

1. What was your favorite letter and why?
2. How did the author use his imagination?
3. What animals in the book can be found in our backyard? In other countries? Are make-believe?
4. How many letters are in the alphabet? How many consonants and how many vowels?
5. What kinds of other things would make a good ABC book besides animals?

> "Creating a library of your child's books is a great way to show them how important reading is. It will also give them a special place to keep their books and will motivate them to keep pulling books from their own library to read.
>
> www.readingrockets.org

Activities– *Animalia*

I am sending home an entire packet of activities to go along with the book. These activities focus on play, rhyme, and song. With all of the illustrations and letters, it might take a while to read this book together. Do not feel like you have to read it all in one sitting.

I am also including the official Graeme Base website: www.graemebase.com. Here you can find more information on *Animalia*, his other books, and apps.

More Books...

For further reading of alphabet stories, check out:
- *Eating the Alphabet* by Lois Ehlert
- *Alligators All Around* by Maurice Sendak
- *LMNO Peas* by Keith Baker
- *Chicka Chicka Boom Boom* by Bill Martin Jr.

For further reading of books with a winter theme, check out:
- *A Snowy Day* by Ezra Keats
- *Christmas in the Country* by Cynthia Rylant
- *Owl Moon* by Jane Yolen
- *First Snow in the Woods* and *Stranger in the Woods* by Carl Sams

APPENDIX

All the Water in the World Newsletter

Family Literacy Children's Book Club

Poems at Home

Sharing poetry with kids is a great way to highlight language. Poems include humor, interesting words, tongue twisters, and alliteration (the same consonant sound at the beginning of each word). Choral reading of poems, where more than one reads the same thing at the same time, and several re-readings of the same poem also builds fluency.

Start with playful, rhyming poetry about topics that are familiar to your child like animals, food, and bedtime. Nursery rhymes and Mother Goose collections are early favorites.

Nursery rhymes are important for young children because they help develop an ear for our language. Both rhyme and rhythm help kids hear the sounds and syllables in words, which helps kids learn to read!

Taken from:
www.readingrockets.org

K-1st Grades

All the Water in the World
by George Ella Lyon

February
2013

"So please, oh PLEASE, we beg, we pray, Go throw your TV set away, And in its place you can install, A lovely bookshelf on the wall."

— Roald Dahl, *Charlie and the Chocolate Factory*

Wikispace Follow-up

I have a wikispace set up for all of my classes at RB Walter Elementary School. Use this website: www.spenceresl.wikispaces.com to find even more connections to our stories and reading resources.

On the home page, find the Book Club link on the left hand side. Once on this page, scroll down past the calendar to find various links.

Use the author link to learn more about our three authors. Next, our Open Court textbook link offers many resources for each story read in school.

Tumblebooks is a great tool from the Green Free Library. Find all sorts of online books that children can read with some activities.

For Kids: lets kids practice reading skills online through games.

For Parents: websites that offer advice, ideas, and information to keep building young readers at home.

Appendix C

Reading Themes

Finding books that match a theme can help children build background knowledge on many activities and events happening around them. These stories help to inspire other crafts and ideas to work on together at home. It can also help narrow down the choices when choosing books at the local library. Here is a list of themes coming up for the months leading up to the end of school.

February- Groundhog's Day

Valentine's Day

Lincoln's Birthday

President's Day

Washington's Birthday

March- Read Across America

Spring has Sprung

Easter

April- National Poetry Month

Earth Day

Arbor Day

May- Mother's Day

Memorial Day

June-August- Summer Reading Programs

Check online, in the newspaper, and at local libraries to join or participate in programs.

Try this website to find other themes that your child might enjoy.

http://www.startwithabook.org/

"Creating a library of your child's books is a great way to show them how important reading is. It will also give them a special place to keep their books and will motivate them to keep pulling books from their own library to read.

www.readingrockets.org

Image Taken From: skill-guru.com

Discussion Questions– All the Water in the World

During reading or after reading is a great time to ask questions about the story. This helps to improve comprehension. Here are some questions to discuss with the story:

1. What kind of sounds does water make when it rains? What does rain sound like to you?

2. Where in the world do people have to wait for rain to fill the well?

3. What are three ways that we use water?

4. What are some words that rhyme with clean?

5. What body of water is closest to your house? Where does the water go from there?

"We never know the worth of water till the well is dry."

Thomas Fuller

Activities– *All the Water in the World* More Books...

I am sending home an entire packet of activities to go along with the book. This packet has more discussion questions, activities, and research. I am also attaching some examples of poetry to try at home, such as the haiku, concrete poem, and a poem that rhymes. Good luck and have fun!

Read a review of *All the Water in the World* and use the Horn Book website to explore and learn about books for children and young adults.

For further reading of poetry and water stories, check out:

♦ *Rain Rain Rivers* by Uri Shulevitz

♦ *Song of the Water Boatman and Other Pond Poems* by Joyce Sidman

♦ *The Rain Came Down* by David Shannon

♦ *Poetrees* by Douglas Florian

APPENDIX

Teacher Questionnaire

Teacher Development Questionnaire

Please answer the following questions about literacy and the teaching of reading and writing in the classroom.

1. How much responsibility should fall on parents to teach reading and writing in the home?

   _____
   _____
   _____
   _____
   _____
   _____

2. What tools or resources could be given to parents to teach reading and writing in the home?

   _____
   _____
   _____
   _____
   _____
   _____

Appendix D

3. What is one strength you have in the classroom teaching reading and writing?

_____

_____

_____

_____

_____

_____

4. What is one struggle you have in the classroom teaching reading and writing?

_____

_____

_____

_____

_____

_____

5. How could a partnership between parents and teachers be better supported in our schools?

_____

_____

_____

_____

_____

_____

APPENDIX

Parent Questionnaire

Parent Development Questionnaire

Please answer the following questions about literacy and the teaching of reading and writing in the home.

1. How do you support reading and writing in your home?

   _____
   _____
   _____
   _____

2. How could reading and writing be better supported in your home?

   _____
   _____
   _____
   _____

3. What are your expectations for teachers when teaching reading and writing?

   _____
   _____
   _____
   _____

Appendix E

4. What types of reading and writing activities do you enjoy doing as a family?

5. What prompted you to attend the family literacy children's book club?

6. What is your level of awareness about Common Core Standards and how they will affect what is taught, learned, and assessed?

APPENDIX

F

EUREKA Flyer

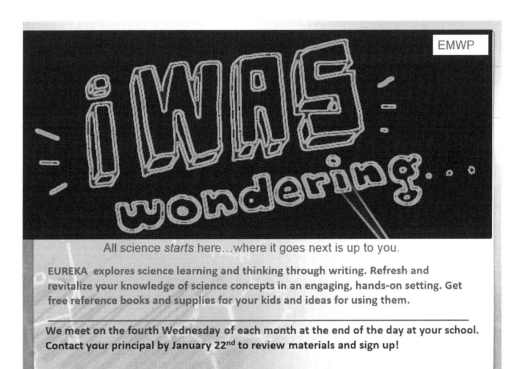

ALSO OF INTEREST

Rebuilding Research Writing
Strategies for Sparking Informational Inquiry
Nanci Werner-Burke,
Karin Knaus,
and Amy Helt DeCamp

Our students must become skilled at finding answers and using information to succeed in college, careers, and daily life. Using inquiry, writing, and technology to infuse passion into the classroom research paper motivates students and results in deeper learning. In this practical, research-based book, authors Werner-Burke, Knaus, and DeCamp encourage you to toss the old index cards and jump-start the classroom research paper so that it is more meaningful, manageable, and effective. Explore innovative ways to help students find engaging topics, collect and evaluate information, and write, rethink, and revise to truly impact their audience. The book is filled with tools and student samples to help you implement the ideas in your own classroom.

©2014 • 144 pages • Pb: 978-0-415-73207-9

SPECIAL FEATURES:
- Clear connections to the Common Core State Standards
- Ready-to-use classroom handouts for different stages of the research process
- A handy appendix featuring a sample research project timeline and rubric
- Helpful examples of real student work and assessments
- Research-based foundations that guide and inform how the process unfolds and why it works

Routledge
Taylor & Francis Group

Routledge... think about it
www.routledge.com/eyeoneducation

Printed by PGSTL